ANCIENT FIRE

ANCIENT FIRE

The Power of Christian Rituals
in Contemporary Worship

Ken Heer

Compliments of...
wesleyan publishing house
P.O. Box 50434
Indianapolis, IN 46250-0434

Call: 800.493.7539 • Fax: 800.788.3535
E-mail: wph@wesleyan.org • Online: www.wesleyan.org/wph
Please send copies of any review or mention.

wesleyan publishing house

Indianapolis, Indiana

Copyright © 2010 by Wesleyan Publishing House
Published by Wesleyan Publishing House
Indianapolis, Indiana 46250
Printed in the United States of America
ISBN 978-0-89827-402-8

Library of Congress Cataloging-in-Publication Data

Heer, Ken.
  Ancient fire : the power of Christian rituals in contemporary worship / Kenneth Heer.
     p. cm.
  Includes bibliographical references (p.   ).
  ISBN 978-0-89827-402-8
  1. Public worship. 2. Ritual. I. Title.

  BV15.H42 2010
  264--dc22
                            2009047992

All Scripture quotations, unless otherwise indicated, are taken from the HOLY BIBLE, NEW INTERNATIONAL VERSION ®. NIV ®. Copyright 1973, 1978, 1984 by the International Bible Society. Used by permission of Zondervan Publishing House. All rights reserved.

Scripture quotations marked (KJV) are taken from the HOLY BIBLE, KING JAMES VERSION.

Scripture quotations marked (NKJV) are taken from the New King James Version. Copyright © 1982 by Thomas Nelson, Inc. Used by permission. All rights reserved.

All rights reserved. No part of this publication may be reproduced, stored in a retrieval system, or transmitted in any form or by any means—electronic, mechanical, photocopy, recording or any other—except for brief quotations in printed reviews, without the prior written permission of the publisher.

"Take from the altars of the past the fire—not the ashes."
—*French Philosopher*

Leading others in worship is a wonderful privilege and an awesome responsibility.
Trivializing worship is a form of idolatry.
Leading worship cannot be handled lightly or approached casually.
There is power in the words we use.
There is life in the things we handle.
There is grace that flows through the sacred rituals and events of the church.

I have offered the bread and wine of the Lord's Supper to
spiritually hungry people, and watched energy flow into their tired spirits.
I have proclaimed redemptive good news to desperate people
and watched the peace of Christ take up residence in them.
I have spoken the final words of committal at the graveside of infants
and watched hope and strength be born again in grieving parent's hearts.
I have joined voice with persons who could no longer contain
the gratitude and praise that needed to be expressed to Almighty God,
and watched the glory of God inspire, energize,
restore, and empower His people.

I have stood amazed in the presence of God as His Holy Spirit
has blown across worshipers, and felt the fire of His presence and power.
And, I have stood, as it seemed, alone in the cold, dead silence
of a worship service that never left the runway to soar in heavenly realms.
I have listened to my own voice bouncing back at me
as an echo of words empty of Spirit and power.
I have mouthed the lyrics of songs sung half-heartedly
that worshiped God neither in spirit nor truth.

I can tell you there is worship that connects with the presence and power of God, and
there is worship that demonstrates more smoke than fire.
And I can tell you which one my heart hungers to experience and
it has nothing to do with resurrecting "the old-time religion,"
but it has everything to do with experiencing the
Ancient Fire in our time.

Contents

Acknowledgements	11
Introduction	13
1. Stoke the Fire	17
2. Remove the Ashes	29
3. Keep the Regulations	47
4. Set Up Stones	57
5. Teach Them How to Worship	77
6. Call on the God Who Answers By Fire	95
7. Avoid Offering Strange Fire	111
8. Add Fuel to the Fire	127
9. Remember the Lamb	141
10. Baptized By Water and Fire	157
11. Fan into Flame the Gift of God	175
12. The Lord Added to Their Number	193
13. The Glory of the Lord Filled the Temple	207
Notes	219
Bibliography	223

Acknowledgements

My worship experiences have been shaped by the influence of two denominations, the several congregations I have pastored, and the vibrant faith and sincere worship practices of multiple individuals. My father was an itinerate evangelist in a conservative denomination that regularly practiced rites such as foot washing and communion within the larger context of "love feasts." I encountered the practices of a wide variety of congregations while accompanying my father in his evangelistic assignments. In my early teen years, my father accepted a pastorate in a different denomination that had its roots in the Methodist tradition and was formed out of the frontier, holiness, and revivalist movements. I pursued my ministerial training and credentialing in this same tradition, where I was then privileged to pastor several churches and serve in denominational leadership assignments.

I will always be grateful for the wonderful people of God I was honored to pastor—including rural, small town, city, suburban, and university campus settings. Each had different patterns of worship, appreciation of traditional rituals, and style preferences. Each taught me to stretch my own acceptance of new worship practices that were not necessarily my personal preferences.

I thank my loving wife, Nancy, for her support of my ministry and the appreciation for music that she brought to me and to the congregations in which we ministered. Her personal devotional practices and appreciation of corporate worship have been an inspiration to me.

Introduction

Opening my Sunday paper before heading out to church, I noticed a front page story that caught my attention. The article began:

> The priest is wearing a collar but has ditched the bright robes of a cleric for blue jeans and a black shirt. There are still hallelujahs in the hymn book, but there's no organ. And the choirboys are missing in action. And while a sermon is in the offing, don't look for the preacher to ascend a lofty perch and deliver the word from on high. Soon, he will be stepping out in the middle of the congregation to take questions. This new take on the Sunday service isn't from some upstart evangelical church. It is an innovation from perhaps the starchiest of all Protestant denominations: the Episcopal Church.[1]

You would have to be sequestered in a cave somewhere not to realize that dramatic changes are happening in the church. While local churches are structuring themselves more missionally and the future of denominations is being questioned, the changes most responsible for rocking the boat are changes in how we worship. Like any change movement, modern worship contains excesses and extremes, along with much that is good and beneficial. One thing we know, though—God *does* care how we worship Him.

At some point, every generation has to make peace with generations who have gone before. Each generation tends to think it is the pinnacle of civilization. We believe we are smarter than those whose organizations, systems, beliefs, values, and rituals we have inherited—not to mention those to whom we will leave our legacy. We carry this mindset into how we do church, often resulting in tensions between generational groups within the congregation.

Most of us have witnessed—or perhaps even experienced—the sting of shrapnel and the wounds of war that often accompany changes in worship patterns and practices. A quick casualty count will verify that friendly fire can be as deadly and devastating as enemy fire. Too often, the worship service—a time set aside for the Body of Christ to connect with God, encourage one another in our walk with Christ, and prepare us for battle with the Enemy—actually causes some people to feel disconnected from God and others and diminishes their ability to wage war against the world's darkness.

Partially motivated by concern that some who feel disenfranchised by the worshiping church never experience this connection and encouragement in the body of Christ, I add my perspective to the hundreds of books written about worship, but with a focus on the *rituals* of worship and how the church might effectively use them to bridge differences and bind together contemporary worshipers.

Two basic concepts form the foundation for this book. The first grows out of a quote attributed to a French philosopher: "Take from the altars of the past the fire—not the ashes." The worship rituals and practices passed down to us contain genuine power—the fire; but they also come with residual elements that retain little value—the ashes. We must retain the central essence of worship and leave behind the residue of worship elements that no longer connect people to God, though they may once have served a purpose. Jesus made a similar distinction when He said new wine requires new wineskins. Leaders of worship must exercise great care and insight to determine what is ash and what is fire. They must be careful not throw out the fire with the ashes. The critical responsibility of those who lead the church in worship is to keep the fire.

The second concept this book is founded on grows out of God's assignment to Aaron and the priests to tend the fire on the altar. God said, "The fire must be kept burning on the altar continuously; it must not go out" (Lev. 6:13). God outlined His plan for the construction of the Tent of Meeting—the place where He would meet and connect with His people—and then prescribed the ritual that would take place at those meetings. The priests were given the responsibility for making it happen. The climax of this ritual was the offering of a sacrifice on the altar; the priests were to be sure the fire on that altar never went out. This requirement to maintain the perpetual fire is repeated numerous times in Scripture, emphasizing the seriousness of God's command. The analogy to present-day worship is easy to see; we must not allow the fire of genuine worship to be extinguished in our churches.

I do not pretend to have the answer that will erase the significant tensions arising from generational worship preferences. However, while navigating some of the current worship whitewater, I do hope to offer a way forward—a means of separating ashes from fire and expressing eternal values in ways that connect contemporary worshipers with God.

I personally dislike attempts to categorize styles of worship by placing them into boxes labeled traditional, contemporary, and blended. These labels may loosely identify a group's worship style, but the terms mean different things to different people, so they require interpretation, which often confuses matters even more. When I use the word *contemporary*, I am referring only to a point in time—current rather than ancient—and to people who reflect the characteristics and complexities of our present age. Regardless of worship style, our mission fails if we do not connect with our present age for Christ. We cannot be effective if we cease to be contemporary. If a church is to be missional, it must always be relevant. God is as relevant as this morning's sunrise, and the church must be too.

From Moses and the burning bush to the flaming tongues on the heads of the followers of Christ in the upper room, fire is a symbol in Scripture of the presence and power of God. John the Baptist said of Jesus: "He will baptize you with the Holy Spirit and with fire" (Luke 3:16). Those who gathered in the upper room on Pentecost "saw what seemed to be tongues of fire that separated and came to rest on each of them. All of them were filled with the Holy Spirit" (Acts 2:3–4). Fire is an image of vitality, but its very nature also implies a caution—fire can go out if not properly tended. Paul admonished believers to "not put out the Spirit's fire" (1 Thess. 5:19). The message God gave the ancient priests is the message He gives to contemporary worship leaders: The fire must be kept continuously burning—it must not go out.

The *Ancient Fire* must be present in our contemporary worship patterns and practices if the church is to exist as a vital force in our world during an age of unprecedented change.

ONE

"The fire must be kept burning on the altar continuously; it must not go out." —Lev. 6:13

Stoke

the Fire

Each generation and culture develops worship patterns that connect them with God. Whatever our differences in worship preferences, we must never lose the dynamic presence and power of God in our worship. If we do, our gathering will have nothing more to offer than a civic or social event.

The chill of the cool, damp morning gripped me as I walked through Arlington National Cemetery. It was not an eerie silence that surrounded me, but more of a dignified hush. Quietness is appropriate in this two-hundred-acre garden of memory. The army of small, white crosses stand at rigid attention as they stretch across the rolling carpet of manicured grass. I had come here to soak in the emotion of the place, along with a desire to see the Iwo Jima monument and the Tomb of the Unknown Soldier. And then, more by accident than design, I came upon the burial place of President John F. Kennedy. The cordoned-off burial site was a simple place—slabs of stone embedded in the ground, some with quotes from the president's speeches etched in them. A large round stone was in the center, out of which protruded a lone flickering flame—the eternal flame—a fiery monument to a fallen leader.

The flame was lit by the president's widow at his burial, and mechanisms were put in place to ensure the flame would not go out. In 1964, the U.S. Postal Service placed an image of the eternal flame on the postage stamp issued to commemorate the assassinated president. The stamp also contained an excerpt from Kennedy's inaugural address: "And the glow from that fire can truly light the world."

The eternal flame at the burial site of President Kennedy is impressive in its simplicity. It invites your imagination to assign symbolism and meaning. It draws you in and momentarily expels the chill and dampness of the cemetery in its warm, flickering embrace.

Centuries ago God chose to reveal himself to humankind through a flame. It started with Moses and a bush in the desert: "There the angel of the LORD appeared to him in flames of fire from within a bush. Moses saw that though the bush was on fire it did not burn up" (Ex. 3:2). God spoke to Moses from the bush and commissioned him to become the leader of God's people—to take them from the slavery of Egypt into a land of promise and blessing. That flame became a companion in the journey, burning on the mountain, guiding in the night, and consuming sacrifices on the altar. That flame was a visible expression of the presence and power of God. God met with them, spoke to them, guided them, and confirmed His presence with them through fire.

> Those who lead God's people in worship are custodians of the flame.

Custodians of the Flame

> Ritual is one of the means for keeping the fire burning—the patterns and practices of worship that connect worshipers with the presence and power of God.

What began with Moses' calling soon involved his brother, Aaron. Moses did not feel qualified to lead God's people. He argued with God about it until God asked Aaron to help Moses get the job done. While Moses was the unquestioned leader—God met with him and told him what to do and how to do it—Aaron became his helper in carrying out God's directions. God assigned Aaron to direct the spiritual life of His people. He was ordained by God to be the first worship leader.

God's word to Aaron, through Moses, was clear and direct:

> The LORD said to Moses: "Give Aaron and his sons this command: 'These are the regulations for the burnt offering: The burnt offering is to remain on the altar hearth throughout the night, till morning, and *the fire must be kept burning on the altar*. The priest shall then put on his linen clothes, with linen undergarments next to his body, and shall *remove the ashes of the burnt offering* that the fire has consumed on the altar and place them beside the altar. Then he is to take off these clothes and put on others, and carry the ashes outside the camp to a place that is ceremonially clean. The *fire on the altar must be kept burning*; it must not go out. Every morning the priest is to add firewood and arrange the burnt offering on the fire and burn the fat of the fellowship offerings on it. The fire must be kept burning on the altar continuously; it must not go out.'" (Lev. 6:8–13, emphasis added)

God gave Moses thorough instructions for constructing the tabernacle, or Tent of Meeting, where He would meet with His people. Occupying a prominent place in the tabernacle was an altar—a place where God's people could approach Him with prayer and sacrifices. Relationship with God began at the altar.

Aaron was designated high priest and given the responsibility of organizing and administering tabernacle life. His sons were ordained as priests to carry out the daily sacrifices at the altar. God's instructions about the altar and the sacrifices made on it were very specific, including the solemn assignment of tending the fire on the altar. Fire was essential to offering burnt offerings, and Aaron was never, under any circumstances, to allow the flame to go out. He and his sons were custodians of the flame.

Those who lead God's people in worship are likewise custodians of the flame. We do not need artificial or mechanical means like those supporting the eternal flame in Arlington Cemetery in order to maintain the flame of God in worship. The altar flame is maintained by relational structures rather than mechanical ones. The flame continues as long as God relates dynamically with the worshipers who come to the altar. The worship leader is the point person who provides for the full participation of both God and His people.

Divine Origin of the Flame

The altar fire was not an ordinary fire. This fire had a divine origin which we read about in Leviticus:

> Then Aaron lifted his hands toward the people and blessed them. And having sacrificed the sin offering, the burnt offering

and the fellowship offering, he stepped down. Moses and Aaron then went into the Tent of Meeting. When they came out, they blessed the people; and the glory of the LORD appeared to all the people. Fire came out from the presence of the LORD and consumed the burnt offering and the fat portions on the altar. And when all the people saw it, they shouted for joy and fell facedown. (Lev. 9:22–24)

The fire kindled by Aaron for the burnt offering was replaced with fire that "came out from the presence of the LORD" (v. 24). This fire from God was to be kept burning. A similar phenomenon occurred as Solomon completed the construction of the temple: "When Solomon finished praying, fire came down from heaven and consumed the burnt offering and the sacrifices, and the glory of the LORD filled the temple" (2 Chron. 7:1).

In both of these inaugural events, once the people met God's requirements for the times, places, and means of meeting with Him in worship, God himself provided the fire. He gave people instructions for how to prepare the altar and sacrifice, but He provided the fire to consume the sacrifices on the altar. It was spectacular and awe inspiring, and the people recognized the fire came from God.

The fire that originates with God is to be retained and maintained by the custodians of the flame. Ritual is one of the means for keeping the fire burning—the patterns and practices of worship that connect worshipers with the presence and power of God. Ritual should not be thought of as lifeless, boring, meaningless, or repetitive, but rather as an effective means of communicating God's power and presence among His people.

The Necessity of Ancient Fire

God chose to reveal himself to His people through the element of fire. He spoke through a flaming bush (Ex. 3:4); led by a pillar of fire (Ex. 13:21); descended on Mount Sinai in fire (Ex. 19:18); showed His glory like a consuming fire (Ex. 24:17); refined with His fire (Zech. 13:9); came upon the disciples like tongues of fire (Acts 2:3); will be revealed in blazing fire (2 Thess. 1:7); and will bring judgment by fire (2 Pet. 3:12). God chose the element of fire as a means of revealing himself in our world.

People have always had a fascination with fire. Ancient Greek philosophy identified fire as one of the four classical elements and associated it with the qualities of energy, assertiveness, and passion.[1] Ancient cultures and religions deified fire. Fire is not God, despite the assertions of superstitious cultures, but God characterizes himself with the energizing, consuming, purifying, igniting, lighting, warming nature of fire. If you want to know if God is in something, look for the fire.

God was in the fire on the altar, and He required the sacrifices made to Him to be made by fire. Altar sacrifice had meaning only if fire was present. Likewise, God is at the center of all worship, igniting the worship experience with His presence and filling the worshiper with His Spirit. Genuine worship and the Fire are inseparable. Worship has meaning only if the Ancient Fire is present.

> To keep the fire burning continuously, we must always keep the dynamic presence of God in our lives and in our worship.

The writer to the Hebrews encourages us to come boldly into the presence of God where we can find help in our times of need, and then says that "God is a consuming fire" (Heb. 12:29). Charles B. Williams translates this statement as: "His holiness is the fire that consumes all evil."[2] He is holy, and He purifies all things related to Him. To worship is to be in His holy presence and to be drawn into Him to participate in His nature, His presence, and His power.

To keep the fire burning continuously, we must always keep the dynamic presence of God in our lives and in our worship. If He is not present—if He is not purifying, igniting, warming, refining, leading, speaking, and empowering—then the Fire (divine presence and power) is not present and the fire (passion and spiritual effectiveness) will die.

The greatest responsibility of worship leaders is to make certain the fire keeps burning. Other issues in worship may be important, but they become meaningless if God is not present and people do not connect with Him. Worship leaders can easily become preoccupied with the trappings of worship without experiencing God. We can organize exciting events around the altar without noticing (or perhaps even caring) there is no fire on that altar. Enjoying or appreciating worship is not synonymous with experiencing the presence of God. According to George Barna, "Eight out of every ten believers do not feel they have entered into the presence of God, or experienced a connection with Him, during the worship service."[3] The church will always face the challenge of keeping the fire burning. Fire is dynamic—ever moving, never contained, and always consuming. There will always be pastors who fail to see the fire is dying, because they remain preoccupied with practices and patterns that no longer connect people and God. There will be other pastors who try to solve the problem of lifeless forms and mindless routines in worship by radical change—enflaming the people without restoring the Fire. They

> The greatest responsibility of worship leaders is to make certain the fire keeps burning. Other issues in worship may be important, but they become meaningless if God is not present and people do not connect with Him.

believe the rituals of the church that once carried the Ancient Fire have become archaic and incompatible with contemporary life, so they decide rituals are unnecessary and jettison them. There will be some pastors with greater wisdom, who solve the flickering fire problem by creating new ways of doing things through which the Holy Spirit can connect with contemporary worshipers. They do not want to lose the Ancient Fire, so they shape new wineskins that can contain the essence of the old and communicate its meaning in fresh ways to new generations of worshipers.

Keeping the fire burning in worship is a serious challenge, especially when so many are unaware that the fire is flickering; when so many have resigned themselves to go on with or without the fire; and when so many insist on throwing out past practices without providing new patterns of worship sanctioned by God. However, this is not a day for being pessimistic about worship in the church. There are those who seek to discern how God is connecting and communicating with people today, and they are intentionally finding ways to incorporate worship practices that have the fire of God in them.

Ancient Fire is the reason for worship. Without it, our meetings are little more than mediocre social gatherings. We must renew our commitment to keep the fire burning and never let it go out.

Reflection

- On a scale of one to ten (ten being highest), how would you rate your current worship experience in terms of connecting with God?

- What worship patterns do you remember experiencing in your formative years? Which were most meaningful to you? Can you identify why they were meaningful?

- When was the last time you felt you really connected with God during worship? How would you explain that time of experiencing of God? Was there any specific act or moment of worship that contributed to this experience?

Moving Forward

- Analyze your worship services and outline your normal way of organizing the service. Make a note of the rituals that reoccur and determine if they are really communicating with the people and connecting them to God.

- Make planning, leading, and experiencing worship serious work for you, your staff, and the people of your congregation.

TWO

"The priest shall then put on his linen clothes, with linen undergarments next to his body, and shall remove the ashes of the burnt offering that the fire has consumed on the altar." —Lev. 6:10

Remove the Ashes

God embodies both constancy and change. His nature never changes, but how He chooses to work in our lives and our world is always subject to change. Releasing our hold on patterns and practices of worship we have grown accustomed to may be difficult and disruptive, but it is necessary if they no longer have the fire of God's presence and power in them, or no longer effectively facilitate our collective worship of God.

Ash is the residue of fire. It is what is left after fire has consumed its source of energy. Wherever there is fire, there will be ashes. Ash was the natural by-product of the practice of altar worship. In addition to keeping the fire burning, the priests were expected to remove the ashes left on the altar after the fire consumed the sacrifices. These two tasks were primary responsibilities—keep the fire burning and remove the ashes. These two responsibilities are inseparable. You can't do the one without doing the other.

When I was a kid, we had a Warm Morning coal-burning stove in the center of our house. Since my bedroom window had a sizeable crack around the frame where snow would blow in during the night, I always welcomed the morning when I could run downstairs and snuggle up to the stove. One of my chores each evening was to stoke up the stove, so the fire would last throughout the night and we could have some semblance of a warm morning. Before going to bed, I had to separate the burning coal and the coal that still had potential for burning from the ash that was left over. Some of the ash settled down into the tray in the bottom of the stove, but I also had to shake out the ashes that remained in the fire box. I would insert the crank into the grates and rock them back and forth to dislodge the ash, leaving only the coal that could still contribute to the night-long fire. I didn't like the ash removing chore, but I understood that too much ash left in the stove would eventually cause the fire to go out. The thought of having no fire in the morning was motivation enough to faithfully discharge my duty.

> Ash is the residue of fire. It is what is left after fire has consumed its source of energy. Wherever there is fire, there will be ashes.

God chose the persons who would be the worship leaders for His people and then instructed Moses regarding their responsibilities, which included keeping the fire burning (Lev. 6:12) and removing the ashes (Lev. 6:10).

These early spiritual leaders were assigned two tasks by God—to continuously tend the fire and to carefully handle the ashes. They had other things to do, but these two things were spelled out carefully by God on several occasions.

A Challenging Task

Leaders must periodically shake the ashes out of their organizations and operations—a task that can be difficult and painful. We want to cling to things that have carried the fire in the past, even though they may no longer serve a vital role in the corporate spiritual experience.

The Need for Caution

Removing the ashes of obsolete church practices, particularly those relating to worship, is often considered too painful because:

- *People* are involved, and we don't want them to be hurt or discouraged;
- *Practices* are involved that we have grown to love, even if we know they are ineffective; and
- *Preferences* are involved that have taken on a sense of the sacred with us.

If left alone, ashes can smoother the fire. When we hang on to practices of the past that no longer serve to fulfill our mission, they can end up putting out the fire. On the other hand, when we attempt to remove elements from worship without regard for their present and future value, we can end up carrying the fire out with the ash. It takes great discernment and grace to remove the ash while retaining the fire.

Some people seem to thrive on shaking out the ashes—in fact they may like to do it too much. They demonstrate little appreciation for the contributions made by past patterns and practices. They have little regard for those who have difficulty letting go of practices that have meant so much to them and others in the past. They become preoccupied with getting rid of anything that carries the scent of the past, and if not careful, they will carry out the fire with the ash. I have little patience with those who are on a mission of change but are not able to articulate why change is necessary, the extent of change needed, or the new reality change will bring about. These change-for-change's-sake persons usually have no attachment to the past and will fight with anyone who does. To them, ash is the enemy—and most things in the church look like ash to them.

Dealing with the ashes from altar worship is an occupational hazard for leaders in the church, whether it is from holding on to ineffective practices of the past or from forsaking what those past practices represent, regardless of how sacred previous generations of worshipers considered them. Either extreme can cause the fire to be lost.

The Need for Diligence

The Old Testament motif for the life of God in the worship experience is fire—a symbol of the presence and power of God. The New Testament motif for the life of God in the worship experience is wine—a symbol of the life and activity of the Holy Spirit within the human spirit. Both carry the image of dynamic vitality, and both carry an implied caution. Fire can go out if not properly tended and wine can be lost if not stored in a proper container. Fire can be smothered by ashes. Wine can be leaked through hardened, cracked, aged wineskins. Both images suggest that there are practices and containers of the divine that over time become hindrances to dynamic connection with the God of fire and of new wine.

> Keep the fire burning and remove the ashes. These two responsibilities are inseparable. You can't do the one without doing the other.

The church has always faced the challenge of maintaining a spiritually alive worshiping assembly in which the fire never goes out and the wine is never lost. But while maintaining the fire, ash is an inevitable by-product. And while retaining the wine, wineskins inevitably become old and need to be discarded for new containers.

Pastors have a lot of responsibilities, and the tasks and expectations seem to grow daily. But pastors cannot escape the responsibility of giving attention to the fire and the ash. As stated in the previous chapter, a French philosopher is credited with saying: "Take from the altars of the past the fire—not the ashes." This is the great challenge for leaders—to carry the fire into tomorrow's worship rather than the ashes from yesterday's fire.

The Need for Sensitivity

My wife and I recently moved from our home of seventeen years to a townhouse which has less storage space for the stuff we have accumulated. I now believe people should move every three to five years just as a matter of principle. We had to go through the painful task of deciding what to take with us and what to leave behind. Deciding what was essential to our new life in a new place was not easy, but the more difficult task was actually disposing of things once cherished. However, we knew it had to be done if we were going to move into our new future. The stuff given weekly to the trash man increased dramatically—because we were on the move. The local Goodwill store became the proud recipient of stuff too good to throw away but not essential to life in the new townhouse. It was hard to let go of some things. There was a time each accumulated thing was a useful and important part of our lives. The process of sorting and tossing also uncovered the reality that different perspectives existed between my wife and me as to what was essential for the future. It is not necessary to

> It takes great discernment and grace to remove the ash while retaining the fire.

go into detail about the different perspectives or whose perspective ultimately won. I simply suggest that the line between trash and treasure is often a matter of perspective and preference. We may want to assign theological or sacred significance to our worship preferences, but usually they do not rise to that level. However, that does not diminish the passion we have for our preferences, any more than our preference for chocolate cake rather than broccoli is diminished by knowing broccoli is better for us. We all have tastes we want satisfied, and we know what we like and don't like.

Our preferences are usually developed over time as our personality, experience, culture, and training generate what we like and what we are comfortable with. Our preferences then create the framework for our perspective on a matter. Perspectives, once engrained in us, become extremely resistant to change. Battles are inevitable when pastors make sudden and significant changes to worship practices, since people typically assign sacred value to their preferences. Pastors must first lead their people to appreciate and accept the new practices that will replace their preferences. Battles are not inevitable; they can, with Spirit-guided sensitivity, be prevented.

A Tale of Two Churches

I pastored a church in a picturesque country setting at a time when it was closing in on one century of significant ministry in its community. The church's rich history was reflected out back, behind the church, where grave stones in the cemetery carried the names of significant denominational leaders of past generations. A major remodel of the exterior was done several years previous to my arrival, but other than that, little had changed with the passage of time. Inside, on the wall behind the pulpit, was a rather rough-sawn cross, complete with knot holes and blemishes. Like other things cherished, the cross had a story. An old hickory tree stood outside and the old-timers remembered tying their horses' reins to the tree. When the tree died, they had a local mill to cut the log into timbers from which they fashioned the cross. Every service they sat facing the cross that carried a silent message of connection with a cherished past. It had meaning to those who lived through the history of that place. That cross symbolized the preferences and orientation of the church. Their worship rituals supported everything that cross embodied. They cherished and clung to their old rugged cross.

Not far from where I presently live is a much newer church that reflects a completely different orientation. At the front of that church is a shiny, metal cross that has been crafted with beveled-edged arms that extend with ends that are pointed. The cross is anything but an old rugged cross. It is modern. It glistens as it reflects the sanctuary lights and the shafts of sunlight that make their way through the chancel windows. It reflects the preferences and orientation of the church. Their worship rituals support everything that cross embodies.

> This is the great challenge for leaders—to carry the fire into tomorrow's worship rather than the ashes from yesterday's fire.

Both churches are committed to Christ and to reaching their communities with the gospel. Their preferences are expressed in the way they worship and the way they go about ministering to their communities. One is more internally focused and the other more externally focused. One celebrates its past and the other anticipates its future. Both churches have wonderful, godly people in them; they are just different.

We have to allow for the differences that exist in churches, people, and the context in which they minister. At the same time, if our history restricts progress; if our worship patterns no longer communicate meaning; if our people would rather die than change; if new spiritual births are never experienced or welcomed in our church; then whatever hinders God's work in us has become ash that is killing the fire. There is little life or warmth found by gathering around the ashes of what once was a blazing fire.

Something is not good because it is old or bad because it is new. And, something is not good because it is new or bad because it is old. The new is not always better, but the old is not always better either. We know this, but it can be so hard to accept it.

The critical task of leaders is to determine what is fire and what is ash, and when dealing with matters of worship, it is not easy to decide what goes with you into the future and what needs to be left behind. Having made that determination, persuading the people to accept your judgment and follow you in making the changes necessary to keep the fire burning is perhaps the greatest task of a leader.

Custodians of the Ashes

The church is rooted in history—a faith history from which we take our direction for the future. However, much of our cherished heritage is often more ash than fire. History shapes our perspectives, patterns, and preferences, but we worship in the present, and it is in the present that we must prepare for the future. Not everything that served us in the past can effectively carry us into the future.

Recognizing the Residue

Worship practices that once nourished the fire can quickly turn to ash. This happens when:

- our practices no longer communicate meaning;
- our practices become more important than the meaning they are meant to carry;
- our practices are not effectively connecting people with God;
- the obligation to perform the worship practice is of greater importance than actually connecting with God; and
- we are willing to sacrifice relationships and Christian values in order to defend our preferences.

Jesus warned His followers about the tendency to hang on to old wineskins. Our inflexibility can make us reluctant to change the structures that do not allow for the expanding work of the Spirit in the church. The forms that once provided the framework for our practices can become archaic—language that no longer communicates; words without meaning; and rituals that have lost the connection with life. The result is worship that is more ash than fire.

Discerning what, when, and how to change worship patterns is one of the most solemn tasks of those who plan and lead God's people in worship. Too many wars have been started over the ill-conceived discarding of what is considered to be ash by a leader but considered to still be fire by a congregation. At the same time, congregations too often settle for ash and refuse to leave the ash pile, when it is obvious that fire no longer is present in their practices.

Samuel Chadwick, Methodist, pastor, revivalist, and educator, wrote in *The Way to Pentecost*:

> The soul's safety is in its heat. Truth without enthusiasm, morality without emotion, ritual without soul, make for a Church without power. Destitute of the Fire of God, nothing else counts; possessing Fire, nothing else matters . . . External

conventionality and correct observance may make a Pharisee, but never a Christian. It is by a holy passion kindled in the Soul we live the life of God. Truth without enthusiasm, morality without emotion, ritual without soul, are the things Christ unsparingly condemned. Destitute of fire they are nothing more than a godless philosophy, an ethical system, and a superstition. Moral and spiritual passion is the essence of the religion of Christ.[1]

Respecting the Residue

Ash is not bad, unless it replaces God as the object of our worship or hinders His connection with people. Ash is the evidence of past fire, even if it cannot be the fuel for future fires. God instructed the priests to be respectful custodians of the ash as well as responsible tenders of the fire. The ashes were not to be handled carelessly or irreverently, but were to be gathered up and taken to a ceremonially clean place by priests who had spiritually prepared themselves to do so.

> The new is not always better, but the old is not always better either.

The ash had been the means of grace and salvation for those redeemed by the sacrifice, and they carried sacred meaning. It represented something of a sacred history that called for careful and reverent handling. To distain ashes is to speak irreverently about God's work in the past, which will hinder us as we move into God's work with us in the future.

The Ancient Fire may presently be expressed in different ways, but the ash is what remains after God has consumed what has been previously offered to Him. We move forward by looking through the windshield, not the rearview mirror. But we can lose our way if we do not have an appreciation of how God has visited His people in the past.

Recounting the past activity of God helps fuel the fires of our future. They become markers that point us forward, not campfires around which we huddle. What has happened is important, but the responsibility of leaders is greatest as they focus on the future. Leaders do not just protect; they project.

Releasing the Power

The Holy Spirit and the life He generates cannot be contained in rigid, restrictive structures of our making. Pastors have the wonderful privilege and awesome responsibility of leading their congregations to experience the stimulating, uplifting, and empowering presence of the Holy Spirit on a regular basis through the various activities of the church community. Too often, the fire of Holy Spirit activity has been programmed to fit into ritualistic boxes that have become bushel baskets that hide the light. The fire is lost and the ritual is declared to be un-useful and is discarded.

Conversely, it is possible to try to force the Holy Spirit into new wineskins unfit for His filling, and the new wineskins are discarded as ineffective and undesirable.

> Recounting the past activity of God helps fuel the fires of our future.

The structures, rituals, liturgies, and sacraments intended to convey the presence and power of God can become restrictive, lose touch with life, and lose their meaning. They are considered to be ash and are therefore discarded, but without careful attention, the fire can be thrown out with the ash. Tossing out the old and replacing it with something new and novel does not mean that the Spirit will choose to bless it. Because a worship practice is ancient does not mean it necessarily carries the fire. Because a worship practice is new does not necessarily mean it has the Ancient Fire in it. To the ageless God, old or new has little relevance.

Some cherished worship practices no longer carry the fire. God may have moved on to new ways of connecting with His people. New times may require new means of carrying the meaning that is conveyed in our acts of worship. In Matthew 5, Jesus repeatedly said "You have heard," and He referenced God's Word regarding how they were to relate to Him. Then Jesus followed by saying, "But I tell you . . ." It was not that God had done away with the old rules, but had given them expanded meaning. Relationship with God is not static, but rather dynamic—always growing, developing, and expanding. It should be expected that the means we use for connecting with Him should be dynamic, not static. New wineskins become necessary for carrying new wine.

But Jesus added, "No one after drinking old wine wants the new, for he says, 'The old is better'" (Luke 5:39). After having our thirst satisfied with what was once new wine, our taste for what has now become old can become our preference. "The old is better" always hinders us from following God into fresh movements of His Spirit. Leading people who want to hang on to the ashes of the past takes great spiritual sensitivity and the process can seriously deplete a pastor's physical, emotional, and spiritual energy.

Pastors would do well to establish a worship planning team where spiritually minded persons who represent all segments of the church can pray, think creatively and theologically, and assist in planning the corporate worship experience. Expanding an awareness of the spiritual journeys of others and what their worship preferences are can help everyone appreciate each other, and can help a pastor sidestep some potentially lethal landmines.

While fulfilling the responsibility of carrying out the ashes and keeping the fire burning, pastors should:

- become students of the dynamics of being an agent of change;
- learn the history and context of their our church before making drastic changes;
- develop the relational skills necessary for conflict management;
- think theologically about worship, not just culturally;
- be creative as they seek new ways of connecting people with God; and
- engage the people in planning worship experiences.

Those who come behind us should be able to look at the ash resulting from our worship and see the hand of God. They should be able to have an appreciation of what we held to be sacred and meaningful. As they join with God in the new movement of His Spirit, they may do things differently, but they can find meaning in the things once sacred to us.

Reflection

- What changes have occurred in the structures, patterns, facilities, and means of worship from the time of your parents up to the current time? What do you consider to be the positive outcomes of these changes? Do you see any negative outcomes?

- Are you experiencing any sense of loss in your present worship patterns from what you have known previously?

- How can you lead your church in appropriately commemorating the good things of the past without being chained to past practices that no longer communicate God to contemporary worshipers?

Moving Forward

- Meet with those who have the longest history with your church and learn what you can of the history and practices of the past.

- Give attention to the processes of change so as to appropriately respect and recognize the past.

- Give careful thought to what is expendable and what is essential in your worship patterns. Commit yourself never to sacrifice the essential while discarding the expendable.

- Determine not to leave behind those who feel great loss when their worship preferences are no longer prominent in your worship practices. Give understandable reasons for the changes being made in worship and try to bring everyone along with you. It won't always be possible, but determine not to intentionally alienate and disenfranchise people when bringing change to worship practices.

THREE

> "*These are the regulations* for the burnt offering: The burnt offering is to remain on the altar hearth throughout the night, till morning, and the fire must be kept burning on the altar." —Lev. 6:9, emphasis added

Keep the Regulations

Our jobs include responsibilities, expectations, and accountabilities. We deal with some responsibilities on an as-needed basis and handle other expectations on an if-I-have-time basis. But being accountable for tasks that rise to the level of regulations is completely different, particularly when it is God who makes it a regulation.

Are you too busy to do one more thing? Do you have difficulty scheduling time for your spouse or family? Is there never any time left for yourself? Do you have very little physical or emotional energy left in you for doing another task? Sorry, but God has one more responsibility to add to your to-do list. It is God who is making the request this time, not a well-meaning committee or energy sapping chronic complainer, so you had better listen up.

That is the last thing most pastors need to hear—that there are additional commands that have to be met and regulations that have to be followed. There are already policies and procedures prescribed by the denomination that govern what to do and how to do it. Add to that the growing expectations of the local congregation and the cacophony of cries from a world clamoring for a piece of their time and energy, and most pastors have more on their professional plate than they can stomach. I can hear the groan when it is suggested there is another thing that must be done. Suggestions can be pushed aside and hints can be overlooked, but when someone says there is something you have to do, it cannot be ignored. It calls for either action or reaction, and sometimes it will bring both.

Full Plates

When pastors begin to react negatively to the requirements and expectations of their calling, they might sense they are getting into trouble. With the multitude of responsibilities, the fire inside can begin to smolder. The term *burnout* is used these days to describe the condition. Burnout is defined by Gary McIntosh as "the exhaustion of physical, emotional, mental, and spiritual strength or motivation usually caused by prolonged stress or frustration and inability to appropriate the full spiritual resources of God."[1] Ministry that is most effective comes from the overflow of a pastor's heart. However, there is probably more over work than over flow in most pastors' lives. The desperation that accompanies burnout tells the over-extended pastor there is nothing that can be done to change things; everything that can be done has been done, and there are no more options available.

> Ministry that is most effective comes from the overflow of a pastor's heart.

Expectations for pastors used to be pretty straight forward. They were to preach and provide pastoral care. The preaching task implied giving direction to the worship service, but that was not considered to be a big deal. And pastoral care meant visiting in the homes of parishioners, dropping in at the hospital when someone had surgery, performing marriages, and officiating funerals. Then the role of counselor was added to the pastoral plate. Ministerial education programs ramped up their curriculum so they could equip those called into ministry to be reasonably prepared to preach, teach, care, and counsel. As churches grew in size and became more sophisticated, pastors were expected to be administrators of the business and programs of the church. Add one more course to the curriculum. The focus used to be on developing pastors—those who could preach, disciple, care for persons, and administer programs in the church. The traditional twice-on-Sunday and once-in-the-midweek programming gave way to an ever expanding array of programs intended to meet the needs of an increasingly diverse community with a wide range of felt needs. This programming began a noticeable shift from an emphasis on pastor to an emphasis on leader. In some cases, the pastoral role and title actually became synonymous with being ineffective, bound by *administrivia*, focused on maintenance, and functioning as a chaplain—certainly not with being a leader. Put another item on the plate and another course in the curriculum.

In most settings, pastors' professional plates do not allow them to choose from the smorgasbord of congregational expectations. This is not a pick-what-you-want buffet. The plate must carry a bit of everything—sometimes things that are not obvious or even written in a job description. There are items that individuals have kept in their personal

> Unspoken expectations can ambush unsuspecting pastors and damage what is otherwise a productive ministry.

picnic basket, held over just for you, and they expect you to add them to your plate. These unofficial, and sometimes unverbalized, expectations have tripped up many unsuspecting pastors.

So, if pastors are to fulfill their expected roles, they must be preacher, teacher, counselor, evangelist, administrator, leader, social activist, engaged in the community, ecumenist, model family person, available for denominational assignments, and an occasional personal errand runner and all-around fix-it person. I still remember the elderly lady who became very upset with me, but I didn't know why. When I finally got her to tell me, she informed me that following a recent snow storm, I should have come to her home and shoveled the snow off her sidewalk because that's what her pastor-father did for people in his church. It wouldn't have been a bad thing to do, if I would have had time. But I had never been informed of the expectation, and with everything else I was doing, I didn't think about it. I made note of it for future reference, so I could recruit someone to get it done for her and others like her. Unspoken expectations can ambush unsuspecting pastors and damage what is otherwise a productive ministry.

Rising Expectations

Then a new emphasis and expectation emerged in church life. In the middle of all of the changes to the pastoral role, the entry point for new attendees shifted from Sunday school to the worship service. Televised services of the emerging mega-churches put on pressure for a new and improved version of the Sunday morning worship service. Placing greater emphasis on the worship experience was not bad, but it added a new expectation to the plate of most pastors, which was often unrealistic. Pastors knew they could not compete with the spit-and-polish productions of the mega-churches. Some pastors adopted mega-church models without the resources to do them well, or without the context in which the changed patterns would be received well. They discovered the hard way that while imitation may be the highest form of flattery, it is not always a wise strategy for the imitator.

Over the span of my ministerial career, I have watched the expectations placed upon pastors increase dramatically and ministerial education programs adjust gradually to the changes. But in many cases, the preparation of leaders for the central task of leading worship has lagged behind. Meanwhile, worship wars rage as churches try to find their place in the changing worship landscape.

I don't think my pastoral training was unusual. I met all of the academic requirements for ordination without a single course that focused on worship or on my role as the leader of worship. It was not until I got into graduate studies that I had the opportunity to choose an elective course on worship. I am not faulting the college I attended, but simply pointing out that in the multitude of practical ministry necessities, ministerial preparation programs have seldom given preference to this priority pastoral function.

Busy pastors know important things can suffer a lack of attention when more demanding things use up available time. After spending hours and hours caring for people and administrative details, pastors must then turn their attention to preparing the Sunday sermon. Pastors find themselves ready to enter the pulpit (or at least partially ready), but with very little thought given to the worship service itself. So they justify their lack of preparation for worship by winging it with the rationalization that the Holy Spirit may move more freely within an unplanned, spontaneous worship time. The result of this lack of thoughtful planning can be the production of more ash than fire.

In order to give greater attention to the worship service, many have taken song leaders and proclaimed them to be worship leaders. It may be unfair to generalize, but few of these new worship leaders have been adequately equipped for the task, except for perhaps receiving a few guitar lessons. Worship leaders are in great demand these days. I am regularly asked for recommendations and am often surprised and saddened by the qualifications (or lack thereof) listed in the search request. Sadly, in today's marketplace, stage presence is often a greater consideration than spiritual maturity and theological insight.

Pastoral Rights and Responsibilities

Among the constitutional rights of ministers in my denomination is: "To preach the gospel and in the case of ordained ministers to administer baptism and the Lord's Supper, to *perform all parts of divine worship*, and to solemnize the right of matrimony" (emphasis added).[2] One of the related duties is "To have the general guidance, under the Holy Spirit, of the religious services, including the midweek service, appointing musicians and *cultivating the practice of corporate worship*" (emphasis added).[3] Further, a pastor is defined as one who:

> The result of a lack of thoughtful planning can be the production of more ash than fire.

is called of God and appointed by the Church to serve as the spiritual shepherd, teacher and administrative overseer of the local church, preaching the Word, *directing the worship*, administering the sacraments and ordinances of the Church, taking the comforts of the gospel to the sin-burdened, the sick and the distressed, discipling converts, nurturing and instructing believers, equipping and enabling them for their part in ministry, and serving as chief executive officer in the government of the local church. (emphasis added)[4]

Whether considered a right, a duty, or an inherent part of the calling, pastors have the responsibility of providing for corporate worship. Some tasks may be delegated, but pastors are accountable for what happens at 10:30 a.m. every Sunday morning (or whatever hour or day worship is scheduled). Even if the leadership of worship is delegated, pastors have the responsibility on their ministerial plate of continuous maintenance of the fire and careful removal of the ashes. As they push around the items on the plate, sampling this and that in order to meet the necessities of the moment, the "regulation" of giving leadership to worship should not be shoved to the edges in order to savor something considered more palatable or demanding.

If pastors are to fulfill their responsibilities toward leading effective corporate worship they must:

- prioritize the demands of ministry without neglecting worship planning and preparation;
- resist the temptation to depend on innate ability to make things happen as a substitute for the more spiritual work of giving thoughtful leadership to worship;
- refuse to hide behind the notion that the Holy Spirit works best when there is little or no planning; and
- avoid viewing spontaneity as the highest spiritual gift.

God gave Aaron and his sons the responsibility of leading God's people in the activities that would maintain and develop them as His people. God's commands and regulations that surrounded their relationship with Him were highly prescriptive and He wanted them to get it right. Their future well-being depended on it. Our worship practices may be less prescriptive, but the responsibility of leading God's people in worship is no less imperative.

Reflection

- What are the greatest stress points in your life and ministry?

- If you made a list of your ministerial responsibilities in order of priority, where in that list would preparing for the worship service fall?

- If you are not a pastor, how much time do you think your pastor should spend preparing for the worship service? Or should that responsibility be given to others?

Moving Forward

- Determine how you can make the necessary changes to get more quality time for worship planning. Do a time study and get serious about prioritizing your responsibilies. Schedule chunks of time for personal renewal and worship planning.

FOUR

> "In the future, when your children ask you, 'What do these stones mean?' tell them that the flow of the Jordan was cut off before the ark of the covenant of the Lord."
> —Josh. 4:6-7

Set Up Stones

God uses places, practices, and props to carry meaning of the sacred from one generation to another. Each generation must learn from those who have preceded them so the knowledge and experience of God can be retained. Ritual is a means of communicating the activity of God among His people and can be the means of connecting multiple generations with their faith history.

I recently visited a small country church that was stuck in a time warp. They were wonderful, well-meaning people, but they were doing things that no longer communicated the power and presence of God. They had opening exercises before Sunday school and sang a rather dreary song—not the kind of tune that could clear the morning sludge from vocal cords or awaken a weary soul. A bit more life was demonstrated when everyone who had a birthday that week was asked to come forward and put an offering in the little lighthouse bank while everyone sang a sanctified version of "Happy Birthday." After Sunday school, they called the troops back together for a secretary's report. She read from a battered ledger book and reported how many people were present one year ago that day and what the weather was like. The weather report a year ago was a bit brighter than the comparison of attendance with that of the previous year. I am confident they have been doing this same thing for at least the past fifty years, because that's the way they have always done things.

Transmitting Faith History

Why we do what we do can be as important as *what* we do. Few things cause the fire to leave our worship practices quicker than doing things that have lost their meaning, unless it is doing novel things without knowing why you do them. Frankly, I have grown tired of change just for the sake of change. I am equally tired of not changing things that no one can remember why they were started in the first place. Effective churches periodically do an audit of worship practice in which they ask themselves why things are being done as they are, with a willingness to follow God in the ways He is currently connecting with His people.

It is a challenge to transmit the meaning behind our worship and lifestyle practices from one generation to another. But as challenging as it may be, it is important that faith history be transmitted to the next generation, even if it means changes are necessary to accomplish this. Our faith history includes stories of how God has worked in the past that may give clues to how He will work

> Ritual is a means of communicating the activity of God among His people and can be the means of connecting multiple generations with their faith history.

in the future. Our faith history includes our testimonies of spiritual realities we have experienced in our journeys and theological truths we have discovered that must not be lost as times change. Orthodox Christianity and the spiritual formation of contemporary followers of Christ depend on a knowledge of the past. Worship is an exercise in historical theology.

It was a great moment for God's people when they crossed over the Jordan River to begin the conquest of Canaan. It was more than an historical event—it was a spiritual milestone. It was a synergistic moment of God fulfilling His promise while the people stepped into the chilly waters of obedience. It signaled the faithfulness of God and the willingness of the people to accomplish God's mission for them. This was a moment of faith history that future generations needed to know about and reflect upon, so God instructed Joshua to tell the people:

Why we do what we do can be as important as *what* we do.

> Go over before the ark of the LORD your God into the middle of the Jordan. Each of you is to take up a stone on his shoulder, according to the number of the tribes of the Israelites, to serve as a sign among you. In the future, when your children ask you, "What do these stones mean?" tell them that the flow of the Jordan was cut off before the ark of the covenant of the LORD. When it crossed the Jordan, the waters of the Jordan were cut off. These stones are to be a memorial to the people of Israel forever. (Josh. 4:5–7)

Planning for Spiritual Formation

Worship serves the church as a major component of spiritual formation. The Word of God is read and explained. Biblical principles are identified and applied to daily life. Challenges to spiritual development and opportunities for making life-changing commitments are given. Theological thinking is encouraged and doctrinal truth is affirmed. Information and inspiration join hands to capture mind and spirit. Sacraments are observed and new life is celebrated. Spiritual maturity is modeled and nurturing relationships are facilitated. Spiritual disciplines are encouraged and compassionate care is offered. God is praised and His Spirit enables His people. We can establish a wide range of programs in an effort to move our people toward spiritual maturity—which we need to do. But we should not overlook the power of a dynamic worship service in the spiritual formation of our people.

God established props—physical objects, reoccurring events, and ritualistic practices—to serve as reminders of His action on behalf of His people and to create teaching moments in which curious future generations could have their questions answered through the repeating of the faith history of their parents. The spiritual landscape of God's people is dotted with faith monuments that speak of God's redemptive work with His people. They were signs or markers to guide those who would follow later. God asked Samuel to erect a stone monument and call it Ebenezer ("Thus far has the Lord helped us") as a witness to His help in defeating the Philistines (1 Sam. 7:12). He established feasts, such as Passover and Pentecost, to be perpetually observed so generations would know of His power and goodness. He prescribed ordinances and rituals to be practiced by the people in order to rehearse and transmit the news of His redemptive activities on their behalf throughout history. Not least among these props is the cross—a monument to an event that forever brought transformation to those who will seek its meaning and experience its benefits.

Faith history should not be a dull and dreaded study of archaic practices—stories that are disconnected from present reality or events that carry no meaning relevant to contemporary life. Our spiritual future should find its roots in our past. There is a movement afoot of persons who are finding new realities in worship as they rediscover meaning in ancient practices. Prior to his death, Robert Webber led a movement that has come to be identified as "Ancient-Future" worship. Webber said:

> How do you deliver the authentic faith and great wisdom of the past into the new cultural situation of the twenty-first century? The way into the future, I argue, is not an innovative new start for the church; rather, the road to the future runs through the past. These three matters—roots, connection, and authenticity in a changing world—will help us to maintain continuity with historic Christianity as the church moves forward.[1]

There is danger if the church moves into the future with no understanding of or connection with its past. Spiritual amnesia will cause a loss of direction and momentum into the future.

Embracing Multi-Generational Church

On any given Sunday, a pastor may look into the faces of at least four distinct generations—each with its own set of predispositions, preferences, and perceptions of life and faith. Pastors face the challenge of communicating to all of them in the same service. Rather than trying to mediate a seemingly unavoidable battle of generational preferences, some have established congregations (or separate worship services) designed to appeal to the tastes of specific generations. The strategy is usually well intentioned—to attract an age group that is missing in the existing congregation or who feels their needs are being unmet in the larger congregation, while avoiding going to battle with other age groups in the church. However, a healthy church is a multi-generational church, and the long-term result of separate services for different age groups will create an unhealthy church. Each age group has something to offer to the other, and the contribution of combined generations brings a dynamic to worship that exceeds that of a single generational worship service. It is arrogant of any generation to behave as if it does not need those older or younger. The church must find appropriate means of connecting all age groups with each other and with God without disenfranchising anyone.

> The spiritual landscape of God's people is dotted with faith monuments that speak of God's redemptive work with His people.

The church cannot afford to sacrifice any generation of members in an effort to attract another generation; in the same way, no generation should be sacrificed for the sake of holding on to the preferences of earlier generations.

One means for transmitting faith history, retaining core theology, and connecting generations is the use of ritual.

Establishing Patterns in Worship

Almost every morning I go downstairs, get the newspaper, fix a bowl of instant oatmeal, turn on the TV news, and sit down to begin my day with a snapshot of what is going on in the world. Sometimes I have honey-toasted oats in place of oatmeal. Other times I add a banana or a piece of toast. Changes in the menu are governed more by the mood of the morning than a thoughtful, strategic decision. On Saturdays, my wife and I go for a simple breakfast of eggs and toast at our special place of weekly rendezvous. You could say all this is a ritual—it is the way we customarily do things in the morning. It is patterned, fairly predictable, and purposeful behavior. Others may do it differently, but this is the way we do it.

This is the meaning of ritual—a customary or prescribed pattern of doing things. We all have rituals. They become patterns for meaningful expression of who we are and what we value. Even in our attempts to be individualistic and shun the practices of others, we establish our own patterns. Rituals are an integral part of our lives. Individuals have rituals. Families have them. Clubs and corporations have them too.

Worship Rituals

Ritual is probably never more evident than in our practice of worship. We establish our way of doing it. Others may do it differently, but we express ourselves using particular language, activity, and moods. We generally like the way we do it more than the way others do it—that's why we do it the way we do. Sometimes we change the regular fare a bit, but we kind of like the way we do things on Sunday morning. Sometimes we add the treat of communion or baptism, but those are special times. We are basically oatmeal people. We think we have a heart-healthy spiritual diet. Any change in our pattern is governed more by the mood of the morning than a thoughtful, strategic decision that there is a better way of doing what we do. If threatened, we can aggressively defend the way we do things—

> A healthy church is a multi-generational church, and the long-term result of separate services for different age groups will create an unhealthy church.

particularly if someone says the way we do things is all wrong and they know a better way.

Occasionally skirmishes break out in local churches over how we practice our rituals. These skirmishes are often in response to changes in culture and how the decision makers think we should do things now to be attractive to people who are not yet in church. Unquestionably, culture and how we think we should relate to it has great impact on our rituals, particularly in a market-driven, consumer-oriented culture. We want to give people a bit of *spirituality du jour*—what can we offer today that will satisfy their pallet, even if their tastes are governed more by unregenerate desire than genuine spiritual hunger? As Constance Cherry says, the contemporary church can "No longer assume that catering to their tastes will satisfy their hunger."[2] But growing the church numerically is our mandate and change in how we do things seems to be the order of the day.

Worship Liturgy

Using a broad definition, ritual is how we customarily do things. In a more narrow definition, ritual is the prescribed or customary words or actions we use when we worship. In the broad sense of the word used in this writing, we have ritual in our worship regardless of the style or form our worship may take. How we customarily worship is our ritual and it gives *our* meaning and definition to what we do. The meaning we assign to the acts of worship we customarily observe may be different than the meaning assigned by other worshiping traditions, but we have ritual that carries the meaning we have assigned to it.

Liturgy is closely related to ritual. Ritual—the way we customarily do things—may include liturgy. The word *liturgy* has its origins in classical Greek and means "public work." It usually refers to acts of worship in which the worshiping congregation participates in deliberate, defined ceremony. Many faith groups that have their roots in revivalist, evangelical, or charismatic movements react negatively to the suggestion of ritual and liturgy, viewing them to be too repetitive, inflexible, and formal for Spirit-led worship.

Following Pentecost, followers of Christ "devoted themselves to the apostles' teaching and to the fellowship, to the breaking of bread and to prayer" (Acts 2:42), and Paul encouraged Timothy to devote himself "to the public reading of Scripture, to preaching and to teaching" (1 Tim. 4:13). Ritual definitely existed in New Testament worship, but no liturgy was prescribed, though Peter and Paul left us creedal statements that may have been affirmations of faith used in the early church.

Faith groups are sometimes identified as being liturgical or non-liturgical. Generally, liturgical churches follow a more prescribed pattern of ritual in their worship, often guided by the lectionary—a predetermined schedule of scripture readings arranged in a logical pattern chosen by the particular religious group for the occasions and seasons of the year. The early church adopted a pattern of scripture reading from Jewish practice, so the use of a lectionary-based worship pattern has existed throughout church history and is not the result of a modern liberal conspiracy.

For the most part, non-liturgical churches feel that worship should not be overly structured but more spontaneous and freely responsive to the movement of the Holy Spirit. Responsive readings of Scripture and reciting historic creeds are usually not considered acceptable. Forms and structures are generally thought to inhibit free and vibrant worship in the attempt to worship God in spirit and in truth.

On the other hand, liturgical churches view form and structure as a means of retaining and recounting the story of God's salvation, in an attempt to worship God in spirit and in truth. They attempt to keep people connected to the historic church and the traditions of their faith through readings, recitations, following the aids to worship in the lectionary, and observing the church year. Paul Basden says the goal of liturgical worship is to "bow before the holiness of God in structured reverence."³ Structure is viewed by liturgical churches as a spiritual aid, not a hindrance to the work of the Spirit.

Labels such as *liturgical* and *non-liturgical* can be hindrances as the contemporary church seeks to worship in ways that authentically reflect our faith and connect us with God. The current labels of *traditional* and *contemporary* are far too simplistic to be useful in communicating worship patterns. While pastoring a church plant, I was interviewed by our local newspaper and one of the first questions the reporter wanted an answer to was, "Is your church traditional or contemporary." I knew her understanding of the two terms was limited and that however I responded, I would be placing our church in a box in which I did not want to be. My reply was totally inadequate to the framework she was looking for, but I explained that I always wanted to be "contemporary," in that we were contextually relevant and we communicated in ways that could be understood by our culture. At the same time we had roots in orthodox Christianity and that would be reflected in our programming and worship practices. Our goal was to be both contemporary and traditional. I am sure she had no clue as to what I was explaining. Such are the inadequacies of the labels we try to use.

> The use of ritual is an important means for transmitting faith history, retaining core theology, and connecting generations.

Whether we are a part of a liturgical or non-liturgical tradition may have little to do with the vibrancy of our worship or the genuineness of our connection with God. We must guard against branding others as having lost the Ancient Fire on the basis of our assessment of their worship practices. I reflect a faith tradition within Methodism which had its roots in historic liturgical worship of the Anglican Church, but which was modified significantly by the days of American revivalism, working with social outcasts, the Holiness Movement, and a splattering of fundamentalism. If that is not enough to make us worship schizophrenics, James White further states: "The Methodist tradition is a hybrid tradition that mixes certain Anglican roots with a Free Church attitude. Added to this mix are a good dose of pragmatism and, at least originally, an interest in examples from the early church."[4] My denomination is a product of the Wesleyan and frontier movements with a desire for the vitality of Pentecostalism (minus tongues speaking) and the evangelistic appeal of Willow Creek Community Church and Saddleback Church (though we may criticize their seeker sensitive orientation). We may be a hybrid of traditional and contemporary, and whatever other labels you might want to assign, but we would not consider ourselves to be liturgical.

> The word *liturgy* has its origins in classical Greek and means "public work." It usually refers to acts of worship in which the worshiping congregation participates in deliberate, defined ceremony.

I was recently accosted by a well meaning church member after I had asked the congregation to sing the doxology following the collection of tithes and offerings. This was a normal practice in a previous church I pastored, and I found it very meaningful—even invigorating. However, on this occasion, the man informed me that he would no longer come to our church because he did not want his kids raised in a church that sang Catholic songs. Personal preferences can become spiritual prejudices that run deep and strong. In describing the differences between liturgical and non-liturgical worship, Robert Rayburn has said:

> Many evangelical Christians associate the word "liturgy" with Episcopalian and Roman Catholic churches. It suggests to them a highly structured, formal, and probably lifeless ritual. But the truth is every church has a liturgy. The liturgy is simply the order of things in a worship service. If a church only sings a hymn, takes an offering, offers a prayer, and hears a sermon it has a liturgy. Too often the difference between "liturgical" churches and "non-liturgical" churches is simply that liturgical churches have thought carefully about their worship services and non-liturgical churches haven't.[5]

Rayburn's analysis would probably be disputed by many in non-liturgical churches, but it does demonstrate the differences and prevailing perceptions that exist between traditions.

Our concern should be to keep the fire burning continuously, regardless of the brands put on us by others or that are reflected in our religious heritage. Christina Baldwin has said, "Ritual is the way you carry the presence of the sacred."[6] Ritual is a means of carrying the flame, but should not take prominence over the flame. The fire is lost when adherence to the ritual becomes more important than the meaning it is to carry. However, to suggest that ritual is inherently bad will be to neglect a means of carrying the flame that can ignite the fire on the altar of our worship.

Someone once described liturgy as "a map for the soul to follow through worship." My wife has accused me of not consulting maps or stopping to get directions when we are traveling. I confess that on a couple of occasions this failure has resulted in not knowing where I was—which does not mean I was lost; I just didn't know where I was. People differ in their opinion about the need for a map to help them in their spiritual journey. The important thing to them is that we make the trip and reach our destination. However, it is possible that if you check the liturgical map followed by another traveler you may find that it will take you through territory you have never seen or appreciated before. The fire of God may be discovered where you did not expect to see it. In a spiritual watershed moment, the prophet Elisha prayed for his servant, "'O LORD, open his eyes so he may see.' Then the LORD opened the servant's eyes, and he looked and saw the hills full of horses and chariots of fire all around Elisha" (2 Kings 6:17). Ancient ritual may open our eyes so we see spiritual realities not noticed before. Our preference may be to stick with the interstate where people like us travel. The joy of the trip may be enhanced by occasionally getting off and driving through roads less traveled and finding ourselves informed and enriched by the spiritual life found along them.

The Value of Meaningful Ritual

Ritual, when used appropriately, can provide guiding principles and practices for our worship, without which our worship can easily become shallow and misdirected. There is value in including meaningful ritual in worship. Its practice may help us to:

- connect our congregation to their faith history,
- enhance our praise through recognition of God's presence and activity in the past,
- keep rooted in orthodoxy and in our core theology,
- build a faith community,
- maintain focus in our worship,
- facilitate progressive order in our services,
- engage more of the senses in worship,
- encourage participation,

- nurture the spiritual formation of our people, and
- escape the trivialization of the sacred that often accompanies novelty.

If we declare ourselves to be free from any ritual, we need to recognize the dangers that may accompany our position. Some of those dangers include:

- spiritual immaturity of our people,
- departure from the theological roots of historic Christianity,
- failure to engage the mind along with the heart and emotions,
- loss of some of the aesthetics that can enhance worship, and
- perpetuating activity that has lost meaning or reason.

Affirmation of Faith and Creeds

There is value in occasionally leading your congregation in affirming its core theology by reading together an affirmation of faith or one of the creeds of orthodox Christianity. It doesn't have to happen every Sunday, but if it never happens, your people are missing an opportunity to identify themselves theologically and declare themselves to be living within their own faith history. The Apostles' Creed is a creedal statement that is accepted by most religious traditions. Shorter statements are available, often composed by denominations for use by their churches. Or a spiritually mature, theologically minded, articulate writer in your church may provide a creative, fresh statement that fits your people and connects them with

> Liturgical churches view form and structure as a means of retaining and recounting the story of God's salvation in an attempt to worship God in spirit and in truth.

the larger stream of orthodox Christianity. There can be power in reminding yourself of your core beliefs and declaring them publicly with others who share them. It is one more place for individuals to participate in the worship experience in ways that build faith and strengthen conviction.

Scripture Reading

Jewish synagogue worship focused on the reading of the Torah, the compilation of Old Testament words from God. The reading was followed by teaching about the meaning of that word. It was this practice that gave rise to Jesus standing in the synagogue of His hometown, Nazareth, and announcing His mission (Luke 4:16–21). The Christian church continued this practice of reading the Scripture and then expounding on that word by means of the sermon. However, the reading of Scripture is often absent in contemporary worship and expositional preaching has given way to other modes. For many people, the Scripture they hear in the worship service is the only Scripture they will hear all week. If they don't read it on Sunday, they don't read it ever. If they don't hear it on Sunday, they will not hear it ever. It is time for a thoughtful, intentional return to reading Scripture in our worship services. We talk about the power of the Word of God to transform lives, but then we rely on the power of our words rather than His.

> Ritual is a means of carrying the flame, but should not take prominence over the flame. The fire is lost when adherence to the ritual becomes more important than the meaning it is to carry.

Reading Scripture should be a ritual that is done with appropriate energy and sensitivity to the spirit behind the words. Responsive reading, antiphonal reading, choral reading, or solo readings by individuals can all be used effectively to allow the truth of God's word to impact those who hear it.

Testimony

Don't overlook the power of an individual's testimony of his or her encounter with God. Few things can energize God's people more than hearing people witness to the saving grace of God recently experienced in their lives, or to hear of the adequacy of the grace of God from a person known to be experiencing hardship, or to learn of the spiritual journey and radical transformation of a person of whose history you were not aware. Testimony time may not take the same form as in past times, but well-chosen words from people who need to let others know what God has done in their lives can be a powerful thing. I have recently witnessed several occasions where the testimony time consisted of cardboard testimonies. People used a piece of cardboard on which they wrote a before statement on the front of the cardboard and an after statement on the back—something that characterized their lives before they accepted Christ and something that now characterizes their lives. I was amazed at how moving such a simple thing could be, but witnessing a life genuinely transformed by God's grace is always moving. Give changed people a voice and you will soon hear more voices praising God for what He is doing. This might even be a good time to reinvent the lay witness mission of past years when lay persons went to other churches and sparked revival fires by testifying to God's work in their lives. It only takes a little spark to get a fire going. Start it in your own church. We say God can transform lives, and it is powerful to let those who have been transformed witness about how God did it in their lives.

Our worship services should include teachable moments when the question, "What does this mean?" though not even verbalized, is answered by connecting the contemporary worshiper to the activity of God in the past through meaningful ritual.

Reflection

- How much time does the average person in your church spend in the ministries of the church each week? How much of that time is spent in communicating the core beliefs of Christian faith?

- During worship, which activities communicate faith history to the younger generations?

- How is ritual used in your church to affirm the faith of your spiritual tradition?

- Is your worship categorized as being structured or spontaneous? Why is it like it is?

Moving Forward

- Read worship resources produced by your denomination or by other faith groups that can provide you with new ways of doing things.

- When you schedule your vacation, plan to visit a church of a different worship tradition and make note of those things that are meaningful that could be adapted to your setting to enrich your worship.

- Identify the generations represented in your church. Meet with key persons from each generation and seek to learn how your worship service might more adequately engage the different generations and unify them in the experience of worship.

FIVE

> "So one of the priests who had been exiled from Samaria came to live in Bethel and *taught them how to worship the Lord*."
> —2 Kings 17:28, emphasis added

Teach Them How to Worship

Worship is like riding a bicycle, right? Once you get the hang of it you never forget how. Once you have done it, worship just happens without a lot of thought and without the need for anyone to tell you how to do it, right? Not according to biblical history.

As the people of Israel were preparing to enter the land of Canaan, God warned Moses about the tendency of forgetting how to worship Him. God said that when they possessed the land of Canaan, they were not to worship the gods of the nations they were dispossessing (Deut. 12:2); they were not to worship Him in the way the Canaanites worshiped their gods (12:4); they were to worship God in the place that He chose (12:5); and they were not to worship in whatever way they pleased (12:8). They were to totally destroy any reminders of the worship practices of the inhabitants of the land lest they be influenced by them. What they worshiped and how they worshiped could be lost under the influence of culture and spiritual drift.

The life of the people of God was to be shaped by the guiding principles of ten major commandments (Ex. 20). The first four of those commandments related to acknowledging and worshiping God. It was necessary for God to give these commands because other things could take His place and diminish the people's reverence for His name. They would be tempted to disregard the Sabbath day of rest and worship or to replace the worship rituals prescribed by God with activities of their own making, even as they lived in a land that itself was a testimony of God's goodness and faithfulness. Both the commitment to worship God alone and the means of worshiping Him appropriately could be forgotten—and they were forgotten several times over the course of their history.

It was even more difficult to maintain dynamic worship practices when the people of God lived as exiles in a culture that was not oriented toward God. They forgot how to worship God appropriately during their captivity and exile to Assyria and when they later resettled in their own land. The scriptural record says:

> It was reported to the king of Assyria: "The people you deported and resettled in the towns of Samaria do not know what the god of that country requires. He has sent lions among them, which are killing them off, because the people do not know what he requires." Then the king of Assyria gave this order: "Have one of the priests you took captive from Samaria go back to live there and teach the people what the god of the land requires." So one of the priests who had been exiled from Samaria came to live in Bethel and taught them how to worship the LORD. (2 Kings 17:26–28)

The requirements for worshiping God had been forgotten and needed to be taught again. Is it so hard to believe that we allow our culture, which does not encourage commitment to God, to dilute our worship of God so that we need to be taught again how to worship? Has continued exposure to the gods of our culture caused spiritual drift and a loss of understanding about how to appropriately worship God?

Some would create an artificial separation between the Old Testament and the New Testament as if God completely changed who He was and how He interacted with people. While the transition from law to grace changed how we become children of God, it did not change the nature of God or His expectations regarding how we worship Him. As with matters of salvation, the Old Testament provides principles and patterns for post-New Testament Christians, even if the prescriptive nature of the Old Testament sacrificial system of worship is not retained.

> Celebrating the nature and goodness of God is a part of worship, but so is bowing in His presence, fearing Him, and trembling in recognition of His holiness.

Every pastor could benefit from identifying the requirements God established in the Old Testament for engaging Him in worship, understanding how the principles behind these requirements guide post-New Testament worship, exploring how they have been expressed in time-honoring ritual, and discovering how ritual can add meaning to contemporary worship. So, what are the requirements of God that should inform our worship practices?

Ascending the Holy Hill

The Old Testament was highly prescriptive when it directed the people in their interaction with God in worship. Approaching God was anything but casual. The times for worship were established. The persons, places, and utensils of worship were to be cleansed and sanctified. The sacrifices were to be of the highest quality. The acts of worship were to be followed without deviation. The attitudes and motives of worshiper and priest were to be pure. Only those who had "clean hands and a pure heart" could ascend into the presence of God (Ps. 24:3–4).

While there are practices of worship that differ between cultures and local contexts, there are core principles and elements that transcend these differences. The Nairobi Statement on Worship and Culture said:

> Christian worship relates dynamically to culture in at least four ways. First, it is trans-cultural, the same substance for everyone everywhere, beyond culture. Second, it is contextual, varying according to the local situation (both nature and culture). Third, it is counter-cultural, challenging what is contrary to the Gospel in a given culture. Fourth, it is cross-cultural, making possible sharing between different local cultures.[1]

The Nairobi Statement further stated that the transcendent elements of worship included: "the centrality of the Word, honest prayers offered in the name of Jesus, the proclamation of the full gospel of Christ, the rich celebration of baptism and the Lord's Supper."[2]

The Old Testament identifies several elements of worship that is acceptable to God. There are at least eight expectations that may serve as measuring sticks for the effectiveness of our worship, replacing stylistic preferences or emotional responses that originate more from our personality than from the nature of our connection with God.

Reverence and Awe

Reverence is at the heart of worship: "Worship God acceptably with reverence and awe, for our 'God is a consuming fire'" (Heb 12:28–29). Worship grows out of recognizing who God is, and when that realization dawns upon the human spirit, there is an immediate response of reverence and awe. As Isaiah experienced, you cannot enter into the presence of God without becoming aware of His holiness and your own lack of holiness (Isa. 6). This awareness causes a change in attitude, and perhaps in posture, as suggested in Psalm 95:6–7: "Come, let us bow down in worship, let us kneel before the LORD our Maker; for he is our God and we are the people of his pasture, the flock under his care." One other example is in 1 Chronicles 16:25–30:

> For great is the LORD and most worthy of praise; he is to be feared above all gods. For all the gods of the nations are idols, but the LORD made the heavens. Splendor and majesty are before him; strength and joy in his dwelling place. Ascribe to the LORD, O families of nations, ascribe to the LORD glory and strength, ascribe to the LORD the glory due his name. Bring an offering and come before him; worship the LORD in the splendor of his holiness. Tremble before him, all the earth!

> *Worship grows out of recognizing who God is, and when that realization dawns upon the human spirit, there is an immediate response of reverence and awe.*

Celebrating the nature and goodness of God is a part of worship, but so is bowing in His presence, fearing Him, and trembling in recognition of His holiness. We have all seen and experienced so much that few things create awe anymore. So many things are proclaimed awesome that even God is no longer viewed with awe. We can enter our places of worship with the greatest of casualness. We even promote casualness in attitude, attire, and atmosphere lest anyone be made to feel uncomfortable in our worship. We should never intentionally want anyone to be uncomfortable, but we should recognize the need to be uncomfortable in the presence of God. It is hard to generate reverence and casualness simultaneously. Worship ceases to be worship if God is not revered.

Holiness

God is holy. Those who enter His presence must not only recognize His holiness, but must themselves be holy. When we come to worship, we can only assemble in the name of Jesus, as people whose sins have been covered by His blood. God told Moses that He would meet His people at the mercy seat—the covering of the Ark of the Covenant between the outstretched wings of the two angels. First John 2:2 says, "[Jesus] is the atoning sacrifice for our sins." Another translation says that He is the "*propitiation* for our sins" (KJV, emphasis added), which is the same word for the mercy seat in the Old Testament. God meets His people at the place where their sins are covered.

> God is holy. Those who enter His presence must not only recognize His holiness, but must themselves be holy.

Worship is a function of those who have been redeemed by the blood of the Lamb. The unrepentant person is incapable of worship. While the unconverted should not be made to feel excluded from attending our worship service, the acts of worship are to be expressions of the redeemed soul. Worship is not created for the unconverted, but for those who have seen the holiness of God, understand His requirement that only the pure in heart will see Him, and are committed to the transformational work of grace in their lives. A worship service that is designed not to make the unrepentant person uncomfortable probably doesn't qualify as acceptable worship, as far as God is concerned.

Praise

Proclaiming God to be worthy of praise is an indispensable element of worship. As Psalm 100 exhorts:

> Shout for joy to the LORD, all the earth. Worship the LORD with gladness; come before him with joyful songs. Know that the LORD is God. It is he who made us, and we are his; we are his people, the sheep of his pasture. Enter his gates with thanksgiving and his courts with praise; give thanks to him and praise his name. For the LORD is good and his love endures forever; his faithfulness continues through all generations.

> Worship is not created for the unconverted, but for those who have seen the holiness of God, understand His requirement that only the pure in heart will see Him, and are committed to the transformational work of grace in their lives.

Praise is the spontaneous response of the human spirit in recognition of the goodness, love, and faithfulness of God. Praise is expressed through a variety of means, including singing, testifying, and verbalizing our adoration in prayer. The celebrative nature of praise is the other side of the contemplative nature of reverence. Neither can stand alone as acceptable worship. Our praise is only empty, emotional cheerleading if it does not come from a spirit that reverently bows in the presence of a holy God. We characterize a genre of music as "praise and worship" music. We should be sure our praise includes worship by recognizing the holiness of God that prompts reverence.

Thanksgiving

Praise and thanksgiving are conjoined twins in the heart of a worshiper—praising God for who He is and thanking Him for what He has done. Thanksgiving goes beyond words to result in action. Beyond our singing, there are two primary ways in which we express thanksgiving: in the celebration of the Lord's Supper and in our acts of giving. A term often used for the Lord's Supper is *Eucharist*, which means "to give thanks." Paul asked, "Is not the cup of thanksgiving for which we give thanks a participation in the blood of Christ? And is not the bread that we break a participation in the body of Christ?" (1 Cor. 10:16). Communion is more than a memorial service; it is thankful participation in the redemptive work of Christ. Thanksgiving lies behind our act of giving tithes and offerings. Again, Paul said:

> Each man should give what he has decided in his heart to give, not reluctantly or under compulsion, for God loves a cheerful giver. And God is able to make all grace abound to you, so that in all things at all times, having all that you need, you will abound in every good work . . . You will be made rich in every way so that you can be generous on every occasion, and through us your generosity will result in thanksgiving to God. This service that you perform is not only supplying the needs of God's people but is also overflowing in many expressions of thanks to God. (2 Cor. 9:7–8, 11–12)

As important as paying the church light bill might be, the giving of tithes and offerings should never be reduced to ensuring the doors of the church are kept open. Our giving is an inescapable act of worship, as we cheerfully show gratitude for God's blessing by giving to His church and its redemptive mission in the world. The ultimate expression of thanksgiving is made by giving ourselves completely to God as Paul expressed: "I urge you, brothers, in view of God's mercy, to offer your bodies as living sacrifices, holy and pleasing to God—this is your spiritual act of worship" (Rom. 12:1). Acceptable worship includes a spirit of gratitude that results in receiving God's ultimate gift and in giving our ultimate gift—ourselves.

Focus

Worship includes singleness of focus. Acceptable worship is the body, soul, and spirit of people directed exclusively toward God. I was in a worship class when Dr. Clarence "Bud" Bence instructed us to take the printed order of worship at our church the next Sunday and place arrows by the various elements of the service to indicate how the communication was flowing: a horizontal arrow if it was running laterally—us to us or leader to us; an up arrow if it was upwardly vertical—us to God or leader to God; or a down arrow if it was downwardly vertical—God to us. As we studied the results, we noticed that often we were talking to each other when we should have been talking to God. Some acts designed to lift our focus toward God directed focus toward the performer instead.

> Worship is not about gathering together to talk to each other about ourselves, but to talk to God and allow Him to talk to us.

Worship is not about gathering together to talk to each other about ourselves, but to talk to God and allow Him to talk to us. Worship ceases to be worship when the focus is placed on someone or something other than God. Scripture repeatedly tells us to love, serve, obey, and worship God with all our heart. There is exclusivity in the focus of acceptable worship. If our worship is not centered on God, we are not worshiping.

Excellence

God always requires our best. He asked for the best of the flock—healthy, spotless, and perfect. This was not to pit one worshiper against another to see if one could give something better to God than another. Excellence was between each worshiper and God. The poor were to give the best they could give, which would be different from what the wealthy could give. Worship is always about excellence—offering God the best, as indicated in these verses: "Bring the best of the firstfruits of your soil to the house of the LORD your God" (Ex. 23:19); "You must present as the LORD's portion the best and holiest part of everything given to you" (Num. 18:29); any sacrifice offered to God "must be without defect or blemish to be acceptable" (Lev. 22:21); "If an animal has a defect, is lame or blind, or has any serious flaw, you must not sacrifice it to the LORD your God" (Deut. 15:21). My excellence may be different than your excellence, but worship ceases to be acceptable when our offering becomes casual, mediocre, or less than our best.

> Praise is the spontaneous response of the human spirit in recognition of the goodness, love, and faithfulness of God.

Spirit

We are more than physical and emotional creatures. Just because our body shows up on Sunday does not mean we have worshiped. The fact that something was said or done that brought a tear to our eye or a lift to our mood does not mean we have worshiped. Worship is more than gathering at a place, participating in acts of worship, or being made to feel better about ourselves and our place in the world. Worship includes the engagement of our spirit with God—the deepest most intimate part of our being meeting in communion with God the Father. Jesus said, "True worshipers will worship the Father in spirit and truth, for they are the kind of worshipers the Father seeks. God is spirit, and his worshipers must worship in spirit and in truth" (John 4:23–24). The greatest commandment is that we love God with all our heart, soul, mind, and strength (Mark 12:30). Not only are we to show up physically and mentally, but our heart and soul have to become engaged so we connect with God at the core of our being—the center of our affections and spiritual nature. Worship is not acceptable worship if our spirit does not connect with God.

> Acceptable worship is the body, soul, and spirit of people directed exclusively toward God.

Participation

In all of the expectations referenced above, a personal response to the nature or activity of God is implied. Worship is a participating activity, not a sightseeing excursion. Too often, either by design or default, individuals have become spectators during worship, not participants. Worship has lost its essence if it becomes a performance of a few for the benefit of the many. As Constance Cherry says, "Perhaps people in the new century don't need to find their worship style as much as they need to find their worship voice."[3] The meaning of *liturgy* is "the work of the people." Liturgy gives opportunity for individual worshipers to become engaged and to find their voices as they participate in the corporate worship experience. If you think liturgy is too canned, formal, or disconnected to be effective, then get creative and develop some fresh words and ways for people to become participants. Too much of our worship services are taken up with performance and not enough with participation. Worship is not acceptable worship if individuals are not involved.

If you want a grid through which to evaluate the authenticity and effectiveness of your worship, these eight aspects of acceptable worship can provide that. A worship checklist could be:

1. *Awe or reverence*: Did we approach God with reverence?
2. *Holiness*: Were we set apart for God? Were we spiritually prepared to enter His presence?
3. *Praise*: Did we express our praise to God for His goodness, grace, and faithfulness?
4. *Thanksgiving*: Did we acknowledge God's work on our behalf? Did we cheerfully give ourselves and our offerings?
5. *Focus*: Was God the focus of our activity? Was it all about Him?
6. *Excellence*: Did we give Him our best?
7. *Spirit*: Did we engage God in spirit, beyond being physically present and being made to emotionally feel good?
8. *Participation*: Was everyone involved in worship activity or did the many observe the activity of the few?

Music in Worship

It is hard to worship without music. Christians are singing people. The longest book of the Bible is a collection of songs. Music fills the Scriptures and will fill the courts of heaven when redeemed humanity joins with heavenly beings in songs of praise to our Lord and Creator. Music was an important part of temple worship as well as in the New Testament church. Paul indicated that being filled with the Spirit should cause people to: "Speak to one another with psalms, hymns and spiritual songs. Sing and make music in your heart to the Lord, always giving thanks to God the Father for everything, in the name of our Lord Jesus Christ" (Eph. 5:19–20). It is amazing and sad that this important element in our local church worship is often the place where tensions build and emotions erupt over stylistic issues.

It seems that God is not too particular when it comes to the musical instruments we might use to worship Him. The Scriptures include references to harps, lyres, tambourines, cymbals, trumpets, rams' horns, and sistrums (cornet-like instrument, 2 Sam. 6:5). Electronic keyboards did not yet exist or they would probably show up too. Neither did pipe organs, pianos, or accordions for that matter.

No offense intended, but I am not too disappointed that accordions are rarely used in worship music today, but I must say that I sometimes miss the sound of a pipe organ blasting out "And Can I Be?" or "A Mighty Fortress Is Our God." Somewhere along the way, the church adopted the organ as an ordained instrument of worship, and it stuck for centuries, only recently giving way to the electronic keyboard and guitar. I have come to appreciate excellence more than the type of instrument. No instrument has God's special favor. An organ played poorly is not as inspiring or acceptable as any other instrument played well. Musical instruments lend volume and fullness to congregational singing, but nothing tops the sound of inspired human voices lifted in worship and praise—without instruments.

I visited a church that was pastored by a popular author-speaker, not knowing that no musical instruments were used in their worship. It was extremely inspiring to listen to a congregation sing four-part harmony enthusiastically as a vocal offering to God. I think God is most honored and pleased when the human voice, with all of its capacity to express what is deep in the heart, is used to sing His praise.

Singing is a function of the spirit as well as of the vocal cords. We joke about those who may not sing well as making "a joyful sound" unto the Lord. I think the Lord listens to the vibration of the soul as much as that of the vocal cords, and it sounds good to Him. John Wesley advised:

> Above all, sing spiritually. Have an eye to God in every word you sing. Aim at pleasing him more than yourself, or any other creature. In order to do this attend strictly to the sense of what you sing, and see that your heart is not carried away with the sound, but offered to God continually; so shall your singing be such as the Lord will approve here, and reward you when he cometh in the clouds of heaven.[4]

There are people who can sing with technical accuracy or play an instrument with great skill. And there are those who add spirit to their talent—and suddenly worship breaks out. That is when music is at its best. Acceptable worship includes music that releases spirit-generated praise to God.

In a world where people seek to be entertained and so easily are attracted to the fulfillment of felt needs rather than real, spiritual needs, pastors need to teach their people how to worship. In churches where people have lost interest and are lost in lifeless ways of doing things, pastors need to teach their people how to worship. Worship practices and patterns need to:

- appeal to both cognitive (truth) and affective (spirit) natures of people,
- engage as many of the senses as possible, and
- use visual aids like video clips and PowerPoint presentations as windows to understand and participation.

The disciples watched the prayer life of Jesus and the intimacy He had with the Father. They came to Him and asked Him to teach them to pray (Luke 11:1). We come to Him and say, "Lord, teach us to worship."

Reflection

- Make note of your customary acts of worship. Which of the attitudes or attributes of worship are facilitated by each of the acts?

- Which of the attitudes or attributes of worship are not regularly facilitated? What could be done to change that?

- What happened during your most recent worship service that did not contribute to true worship and could be eliminated in the future?

Moving Forward

- Look for ways to engage more of the senses in worship. Appeal to the aesthetics with visual worship aids. Engage the imagination and energy of your worshipers.

- Use your preaching and other means of teaching to instruct your people in how to worship.

- Establish some visual, experiential markers that can be repeated to keep people connected with meaningful faith exercises. Focus on seasonal emphases where traditions can be anticipated that ground your people in great events of their faith.

SIX

"Then you call on the name of your god, and I will call on the name of the Lord. The god who answers by fire—he is God."
—1 Kings 18:24

Call on the God Who Answers By Fire

It is risky to advertise that the church will meet for worship at 10:30 a.m. on Sunday. If worship involves having a meeting with God, what if He doesn't show up? We can really be embarrassed if we call on God to do something, fully expecting He will intervene and perform the miraculous, but He does not respond. So, rather than be embarrassed, we adjust our expectations downward—unsure that He will show up in any dramatic, undeniably supernatural way. We can be as surprised as anyone else when He shows up, and we do not expect Him.

When God Shows Up

Some people are known as "the faithful"—they show up for worship every week. If they miss a service, you know something serious is wrong and you check on them as soon as you are able. Other people surprise you when they show up. You expect them on Christmas, Easter, and occasionally on a special Sunday, but it concerns you when they just show up unexpectedly. Is there a plan to vote on renewing your call today and no one told you? Is there something going on of which you are not aware? Is the person experiencing some kind of suffering or difficulty in life?

His words went through my heart like a knife. They hurt, not only because I respected the person who said them and considered him a friend, but because I knew what he said was at least partially true. I went to their home that evening because they had let it be known they were growing dissatisfied with our church and were considering changing to another one. I sat in their living room and heard him say they had not felt God in our worship services for some time. I knew that while I carried responsibility for facilitating our congregation's connection with God in worship, they carried some personal responsibility as well for what they felt was lacking. While I could not make it happen myself, as the leader of worship, I carried a major responsibility for creating the environment where God could meet with His people. I was there. The faithful were there. And this couple was there. But it was not obvious to everyone that God was there.

> If God doesn't show up, it really doesn't matter who else does.

It is wonderful when God shows up. Elijah knew the feeling. Ahab, Jezebel, and their henchmen prophets had intimidated God's people long enough. It was time for God to intervene and vindicate himself and His people. So Elijah did a risky thing—he issued a challenge to the heathen prophets in which he put his God to the test. He built an altar and then challenged the pagan prophets: "Let's all call on our god and the one who answers by fire will prove that he is the true God." It would be bad for Elijah if

God did not show up for this event, plus it could be an embarrassment for God.

Years ago, I heard the supposedly true story that on Christmas Eve the telephone rang in the office of the pastor of the church in Washington, D.C., that President Franklin Roosevelt attended. The caller asked if there would be a Christmas Eve service at the church that evening. When he was told there would be, he asked if they expected President Roosevelt to attend the service. The pastor replied, "I can't promise. I'm not sure about the President's plans for this evening. But I can say that we fully expect God to be in our church tonight, and we feel secure in the knowledge that His attendance will attract a reasonably large congregation."[1]

If God doesn't show up, it really doesn't matter who else does. It is good to reconnect with our friends that we haven't seen all week, but they shouldn't be the main attraction. His presence is what turns a meeting of people into a service of worship.

> Let me experience the God who answers by fire, and the label given to the type of worship no longer matters.

We can pack our gang in the car and head to church on Sunday morning with the expectation that God will be there, but is it automatic that God will show up every Sunday just because we do? If He doesn't show, is He missed, or can we go on without Him and enjoy the time just as much? Would we be surprised if He showed up unannounced? We find comfort in the reality that Jesus said if two or three gather in His name, He will be there. Armed with that promise, should we expect to go away from every worship service with the conviction that we have just met with God and His fire has rekindled something in our spirits?

The big question is this: Is our God any different than anyone else's god? Does the God who answers by fire show up when we call on Him?

The answer presupposes that we *call* on Him. It suggests that there are situations of our lives that will be severely diminished if He does not answer our prayer when we come together in the name of Jesus. It is critical to our spiritual survival that we call on God and that He responds by providing resources that are beyond our capacity to generate on our own. A vital part of worship is a declaration of our need for God to show up. Moses said it best when he told God he didn't want to lead the children of Israel toward the land of promise if God did not go with him. Moses said that God's presence was the only thing that separated them from everyone else: "What else will distinguish me and your people from all the other people on the face of the earth?" (Ex. 33:16). We need His presence and we depend on His power, or we are no different than the Rotary Club, the Red Hat Society, or the fans gathered at the local ball game.

We hunger to experience the God who answers by fire. We don't want to waste our time with gods that are hollow imitations of the real thing. We have had enough of the gods of this world that fill our storage barns but leave our souls empty. We quickly grow tired of worship services that may qualify as a mediocre pep rally but never seem to take us into the presence of God. Stylistic differences created by personal preferences can be minimized or marginalized if God is experienced. He is the substance that transcends style preferences. Let me experience the God who answers by fire, and the label given to the type of worship no longer matters. One remedy for our squabbles over worship is to stop fussing about style and start calling on God to visit us.

Every Sunday, we come together to challenge the gods of this world that have accosted us all week long. We dare to call on God and expect Him to show up. Like the wood that surrounded Elijah's altar, our spirits have been soaked by the cold waters of life in a faithless world. We place ourselves on the altar and ask God to set us on fire, and we declare our dependence upon and our confidence in the God who answers by fire. If He doesn't show up, we are in a heap of trouble.

Don't Pass Go

Some things cannot be skipped if we want to get where we want to go. Our worship should begin by calling on God. Traditionally, worship has begun with a call to worship and an invocation. The call to worship is when people are invited into the presence of God. The invocation is when God is invited into the presence of the people.

Call to Worship

Face it: We are not always in the spirit of praise and worship when we take our seat in church. We are not always ready to make the transition from life in the world—even life in the car on the way to church—into life in the presence of God. A call to worship is the bridge from where we are to where we want to be (or need to be) in order to connect with God. It collects our attention that has been fragmented by life's events and establishes our focus, purpose, mood, and anticipation. A call to worship can take the form of a verse of Scripture, a song, an instrumental selection, a drama, a video clip, or a verbal call to come into the presence of God. It is like the hammering of a gavel to get attention, the trumpet call to bring participants to the starting gate, the ringing of a bell to start a class, or a voice calling a meeting to order.

Worship should begin with a call that brings people into the anticipated presence of God. One TV church begins each service with the words, "This is the day that the Lord has made. We will rejoice and be glad in it." These customary words are a signal that the worship service has begun and they have come to be expected. However, you will probably want to vary the call to worship from service to service to help to set the mood you desire or to suit the occasion.

Invocation

A sincere prayer calling for God to be a part of the service announces to everyone that this is to be a spiritual meeting between God and His people. This meeting is to be different from others in which they may have participated in during the week. God is being invited, and He is expected to be present. The call to worship acknowledges His presence and quickens the expectation that He will ignite fire in the hearts of worshipers. To invoke means to call upon, or to summon. The omnipresent God waits to be invited into our lives and our worship. If He is not intentionally invited to come, we probably shouldn't be surprised if He doesn't show up.

Pastoral Prayer

> The omnipresent God waits to be invited into our lives and our worship. If He is not intentionally invited to come, we probably shouldn't be surprised if He doesn't show up.

The pastoral prayer is a time for a pastor to talk to God on behalf of the people. Pastors have many roles that accompany their calling, such as prophet, preacher, teacher, shepherd, and leader. They also function in the role of priest—helping people to connect with God and interceding with God on their behalf. People need to hear their pastor pray for them—not just for the lost, the missionaries, and the governmental leaders—but for them. The pastoral prayer is a ritual that needs to be reemphasized in contemporary worship. It is good to involve lay persons or ministerial staff in various parts of the worship service, but there is power in the connection that takes place between people, priest, and God when pastors pray for their people.

When you pray for your people, it lets them know you are aware of their needs, that you care about the things that trouble them, that you have a connection with the God who answers by fire, and that you make telling God about their needs a prominent part in the worship experience. Without question, you will pray for your people during the private times of prayer throughout the week, but you also need to publicly call on God on their behalf and expect that the God who answers by fire will show up in their lives.

> The man or woman of God is totally dependent upon the enablement and anointing of God.

Calling for people to come forward to accept Christ at the close of a service is becoming rare these days. But people are not all that reticent about acknowledging they have a need and desire others to pray for them by coming forward during the time of public prayer. Their needs may range from a nagging pain to a broken heart, but without question, spiritual needs exist and are often the unspoken reason for seeking prayer. It is a great time for the pastor to move among the seekers, giving an appropriate touch and calling on God to meet each person's need. Why would you want to neglect this wonderful opportunity to facilitate the connection between people with needs and the God who answers by fire?

Prayer for Healing

Wonderful things happen when God's people gather in worship. The body of Christ is made up of people who have been spiritually gifted to assist each other in moving toward maturity and wholeness. There is healing power in the fellowship of believers. When God shows up among His people, miraculous things happen. People are made whole—spiritually, mentally, relationally, and physically. We should "feel" better when we leave church than we did when we went to church.

If believers are sick, they are encouraged to call the elders of the church to anoint them and pray for their healing (James 5:14–16). Prayer for the sick has been a rite of the church since the days of the New Testament. Ritual was established to assist the church in caring for the sick and calling on God to heal them. We are encouraged by God to call on Him with the expectation that He will answer and do what we are incapable of doing. However, too often we shy away from praying for the sick lest we become embarrassed when nothing happens. Churches are returning to this ancient ritual—providing a bit of high touch in a high tech world. People need the touch of faith. People need to know others in the church care about them and are praying for them. People need God to intervene in the struggles of their lives. Why not do what God encourages by announcing a service where there will be prayer for the sick—and then let it become a regular pattern of church life? Call on God and give Him a chance to respond. Let people know that in this place, we call on God with the expectation that He will show up, and people find wholeness here. Above all, the church is a hospital for sick souls, and the Great Physician moves from chair to chair bringing hope and healing to those who seek Him.

The Power of Six

The man or woman of God is totally dependent upon the enablement and anointing of God. Pastors should regularly, routinely, and earnestly call upon God to bring the fire that will make their ministry effective. Others should also be engaged in praying for the minister and the worship service. This is not a mundane, superficial commitment by a few half-hearted pray-ers. Any effectiveness I may have had in my public ministry I owe to a small cadre of men who did battle for me every Sunday morning. There were six spiritually mature men who joined me in my study just before I made my way to the church worship center. I shared with them my concerns for the service, my personal needs, the subject for the morning, what I thought God wanted to accomplish in this service, and how they could be praying during the next hour. They then placed their hands on me and prayed. When I went before my people, I knew God was aware of my dependency upon Him and I knew there were six men holding up my arms. It was a ritual with fire power in it.

Congregational Prayer

Prayer is an indispensible part of congregational life. You might find it difficult to use the words *prayer* and *ritual* in the same sentence, but prayer should be one of those things that is a purposeful, predictable pattern of our worship—a ritual. The ritual of prayer can be offered as the invocation, at the offering, with congregational participation, as a pastoral prayer, and as a closing prayer. Prayers can be thoughtfully written out or given spontaneously. They can be offered by individuals or groups. Concerts of prayer have become meaningful ways for people to participate in public prayer that moves through a progressive journey of subjects, interspersed with Scripture or singing. Concerts of prayer provide for structured spontaneity. Occasionally, encourage people who want others to pray for them to stand, and have others gather around them, place their hands on them, and pray for them. It is powerful when people pray for each other, calling on God and expecting Him to respond.

Offerings

The time of receiving the offering is often approached as a necessary evil—resented by some and seen as a meaningless and lifeless ritual by many. Giving an offering to God is a spiritual act in which we thank God for what we have, but it is also a means of declaring our dependence on Him—calling on Him to provide our daily bread. We are to give God the firstfruits of our labor—before, not after we have used what we need—and then trust that He will provide the "later" fruit we need for essentials. Our offerings are a means of calling on God to show up as we face the challenges of caring for the responsibilities that are legitimately ours. Giving our offering to God is one of the most spiritual things we can do during a worship service, therefore praying before or after the offering is not a trite, meaningless ritual.

We are to give sacrificially. Our sacrifices are different than those given by people in biblical times, but the spirit and costliness of the gift should be the same. We give with the desire that God will consume our sacrifice to His glory. Exodus 29:18 says, "Then burn the entire ram on the altar. It is a burnt offering to the LORD, a pleasing aroma, an offering made to the LORD by fire." Thirty-nine times the Scriptures speak of offerings "made to the Lord by fire." In most of these references, it speaks of the offering being "a pleasing aroma" to God. The God who answers by fire is pleased with offerings made by fire—sacrifices intended for God to consume. If you want God to visit your people, lead them to become sacrificially giving people.

> Giving an offering to God is a spiritual act in which we thank God for what we have, but it is also a means of declaring our dependence on Him—calling on Him to provide our daily bread.

Every church, in one form or another, practices the ritual of receiving an offering every week, and leaders of worship need to give greater thought and attention to it. It is possible to make this a ritual with meaning—eagerly anticipated. Don't try to apologize for receiving the offering or minimize its place in the service. Provide good, solid, spiritual reasons for giving to the work of God. Make giving an upbeat, joyful time. Occasionally make use of a tithing testimony to inspire others in the gift of giving. Feature some of the results of the sacrificial giving of your people so they know their giving, offered as a means of calling on God to meet their needs, has brought a response from the One who answers by fire.

Demonstrations of the presence and power of God are not restricted to past generations. The fire that consumed the sacrifice on Moses' altar appeared again at Solomon's altar and again on Elijah's altar and again on worshipers during Pentecost. Each generation experiences the glory of the Lord when they truly connect with him in dynamic worship. Once you have experienced the fire of the Holy Spirit in worship, you have an insatiable hunger for more.

God's people can hardly wait for Sunday, if they expect to see and experience God there. Call on Him and let Him answer by fire.

Reflection

- How do you customarily begin worship? Is it varied or always the same? What response did you intend to affect in worshipers with the way you began worship last week? Was it effective in bringing God and people into the same time and space?

- How often do you think your people would say they really believe God showed up during worship? Why do you think they would say this?

Moving Forward

- What will you do next week that will help people make the transition from their world into God's world as they enter worship?

- Compile a list of Scripture verses that can help your people to focus on the offering as a spiritual act of worship and use a different one each Sunday.

- Visualize yourself to be a priest who is the connection between God and His people, and the people with their God. Meditate on how you can lead your people in prayer that will help them realize this connection. You do not have to write out a prayer, but make a list of the needs of your people and of the grandness of God and His grace, and how you can bring needy people into the presence of a gracious God.

- Gather a group of spiritually mature people who can pray for you before and during the service. Let them know the focus of your message and how they can specifically ask God to move in the hearts of the people so they will respond obediently to the message.

- Schedule a specific time when prayer will be offered for healing and publicly invite people to bring their brokenness to God to experience His wholeness.

SEVEN

"They made an offering with unauthorized fire." —Num. 3:3

Avoid Offering

Strange Fire

Left to our own devices, we can resort to gathering around bonfires of our own making while we sing "Kum Ba Ya," rather than seeking and experiencing the Ancient Fire. Worship shortcuts and counterfeit fires are plagues that infect too many worship gatherings.

Whenever there is something of value, the creation of a cheaper counterfeit is sure to be lurking in the shadows. There are always those who want to find ways to cash in on the value of something without investing in the genuine, and there will always be those who seek shortcuts to the blessings of God. Man-made fire can generate a lot of attention, but ultimately produces a worship experience that neither honors God nor satisfies the spiritual hunger of seeking hearts.

A massive fire recently destroyed a large housing and commercial development under construction in our city. As soon as the fire was extinguished, investigators moved in to determine the origin of the fire. They were suspicious that a fire that so quickly consumed the complex must have been intentionally set, so they sent in dogs that were trained to sniff out any lingering evidence of the use of an accelerant. Amazingly, within hours the expert investigators determined that an arsonist set the fire and they pinpointed where and how the fire was started. If conditions are right, spontaneous combustion is possible, but usually fires are started intentionally, and evidence will usually point to their origin.

The fire that was to be kept continuously burning on the altar had a divine origin. It was ignited on the altar at the Tent of Meeting:

> Then Aaron lifted his hands toward the people and blessed them. And having sacrificed the sin offering, the burnt offering and the fellowship offering, he stepped down. Moses and Aaron then went into the Tent of Meeting. When they came out, they blessed the people; and the glory of the LORD appeared to all the people. Fire came out from the presence of the LORD and consumed the burnt offering and the fat portions on the altar. And when all the people saw it, they shouted for joy and fell facedown. (Lev. 9:22–24)

And again at the newly constructed temple: "When Solomon finished praying, fire came down from heaven and consumed the burnt offering and the sacrifices, and the glory of the LORD filled the temple" (2 Chron. 7:1).

In both of these inaugural events that established the times, places, and means of meeting with God in worship, God was the originator of the fire on the altar. He provided instructions for people's involvement in the preparation of

> Man-made fire can generate a lot of attention, but ultimately produces a worship experience that neither honors God nor satisfies the spiritual hunger of seeking hearts.

every detail for worship, but ultimately He provided the fire that gave purpose to the events surrounding the altar. That fire-originating event was spectacular and awe inspiring, and the people recognized the fire was God-originated.

Counterfeit Fire

It should not be surprising that immediately following this dramatic demonstration of the presence and power of God, a substitute for divine fire shows up. Aaron had two sons who were ordained to serve as priests, and they shared the responsibility of keeping the fire on the altar burning. It is unclear if they allowed the fire to go out and had to reignite it; if they erected an altar other than the one God had ordained and then started a new fire on it; or if they were not spiritually prepared to make the offering as God had required. In any case, they lit a fire with which God was not pleased. It is recorded in Numbers 3:3–4 and again in 26:61, that Nadab and Abihu died when they made an offering before the Lord with *unauthorized* fire. Other versions translate the word *strange* (KJV) or *profane* (NKJV). Their fire was of their making and was not God's fire. They committed spiritual arson.

> If conditions are right, spontaneous combustion is possible, but usually fires are started intentionally, and evidence will usually point to their origin.

> Aaron's sons Nadab and Abihu took their censers, put fire in them and added incense; and they offered unauthorized fire before the LORD, contrary to his command. So fire came out from the presence of the LORD and consumed them, and they died before the LORD. (Lev 10:1–2)

This time, when the fire of the Lord came, it came to consume those who dared to counterfeit His fire.

Whatever the offence of Nadab and Abihu, it was serious enough for God to take their lives. How you handle the presence of God is serious business. The Israelites were made painfully aware of this on several occasions. Most notably was when Uzzah touched the ark of the covenant as it was returning from the Philistines and being transported back to Judah. The ark was the symbol of God's presence and was the place where He said He would meet with His people, and no one was to touch it. The ark was at the center of the holiest of interactions between God and His people and was to be treated with the highest of respect. Uzzah's violation of God's command to never touch the ark may seem innocent and well-meaning to us, and God's reaction to Uzzah's violation may seem questionable and reactionary to us. But when God struck Uzzah dead, it underscored again how serious our handling of the presence of God is. We are to worship no other god but Him, and share His glory with no one. We are to worship Him alone, and how we worship Him matters.

Unacceptable Worship

Strange fire is unacceptable to God, as Aaron's sons discovered. It would not be consistent with the nature of God to punish them or to reject us for innocently violating unknown requirements of acceptable behavior. Our common definition of sin is: "the willful transgression of a *known* law of God" (emphasis added).[1] So there must be some principles in the Scripture that can guide us in our worship practices so they are not considered by God to be strange, unauthorized, or profane. I suggest a few.

Worship Not Accompanied with Faith

It was demonstrated early in human history that not all acts of worship are created equal or received by God as acceptable. Adam and Eve knew what it meant to walk and talk with God in intimate relationship. They must have instilled in their sons the need to worship God, because after establishing their vocational choices, the first thing recorded about the brothers, Cain and Abel, was that they both made offerings to God. And God responded differently to each of their offerings: "The LORD looked with favor on Abel and his offering, but on Cain and his offering he did not look with favor" (Gen. 4:4–5). Some argue that God's favor or disfavor was because of the nature of the offering; Abel gave "fat portions from some of the first born of his flocks" (suggesting an animal sacrifice, Gen 4:4), and Cain gave "some of the fruits of the soil" (Gen. 4:3). I tend to think the acceptance of the offering was based on the nature of the person making the offering, not the nature of the offering itself. Hebrews 11:4 says, "*By faith* Abel offered God a better sacrifice than Cain did. *By faith* he was commended as a righteous man, when God spoke well of his offerings" (emphasis added). Faith made the sacrifice better, not the nature of the sacrifice. Worship is more than an act that is performed. Faithless people cannot worship. Each person brings who they are and what they have to offer God, but if our acts of worship, however they may differ, are not accompanied by faith, the act becomes unacceptable—strange fire.

Worship Hindered by Human Relationships

Worship is a divine-human experience—an individual connecting with the presence and power of God. But Jesus said our relationship with other people can hinder our relationship with God and make our worship ineffective. If we are disconnected from our brother or sister, we need to mend the fracture before we try to connect with God. Jesus said in Matthew 5:23–24:

> Therefore, if you are offering your gift at the altar and there remember that your brother has something against you, leave your gift there in front of the altar. First go and be reconciled to your brother; then come and offer your gift.

God will not hear us tell Him how great our love is toward Him when we are unable to express our love toward others.

Worship Having Too Much "Us" in It

Worship is all about God, not us. Whenever worship is filtered through the lens of "self" and is engineered to make us look good or to feel better about ourselves, it is impossible to focus on God. Acceptable worship requires moving ourselves off the throne and onto the altar. Paul said, "I urge you, brothers, in view of God's mercy, to offer your bodies as living sacrifices, holy and pleasing to God—this is your spiritual act of worship" (Rom. 12:1). Worship of God requires making a sacrifice of ourselves, only then can it be "spiritual."

Jesus spoke of a Pharisee and a tax collector who went to the temple to pray. The Pharisee "prayed about himself" and bragged to God about how often he fasted, how much he tithed, and how he was better than others. The tax collector simply bowed as a sinner before the holy God and asked for mercy. Jesus said it was the tax collector who connected with God, not the self-justified Pharisee (Luke 18:10–14). God

> Each person brings who they are and what they have to offer God, but if our acts of worship, however they may differ, are not accompanied by faith, the act becomes unacceptable—strange fire.

detests pride, and when there is too much "us" in our worship, our pride turns our worship into strange fire. There can be the unjustified pride of performance, whether demonstrated in music or in the sermon. There can be too much "us" in the do-or-die insistence that our preferences must always be the standard for acceptable worship, and meeting our requirements are more important to us than meeting God's requirements. There can be attachment to other persons that takes on more importance to us than connection with God. In the early church, there were those who followed one leader over another, bragged about being baptized by one person rather than another, and said one preacher was smarter and spoke with greater eloquence than another (1 Cor. 1). This insertion of too much self into worship resulted in a fractured and dysfunctional church that was displeasing to God.

> Worship is all about God, not us. Whenever worship is filtered through the lens of "self" and is engineered to make us look good or to feel better about ourselves, it is impossible to focus on God.

Worship That Satisfies the Physical and Not the Spiritual

Amazingly, Paul went so far as to tell the church at Corinth that their worship services did "more harm than good" (1 Cor. 11:17). Not only were the divisions between them hindering their worship, but they had taken the sacred meal of the Lord and profaned it. Paul told them they were going through the motions of Communion, but "it is not the Lord's Supper you eat" (1 Cor. 11:20). Individuals were so personally absorbed that they had no consideration for others or for the spiritual nature of their acts of worship. They came to eat physical bread, not partake of the spiritual body of the Lord. They came to get drunk on the wine, not partake of the spiritual blood of the Lord. The common elements of bread and wine are consecrated to produce spiritual nourishment in us. They reversed the nature of the sacrament by turning spiritual elements back into common, physical food and drink that were consumed to satisfy physical appetites but which left their spiritual lives malnourished and dying.

Worship That Substitutes Human Passion for Divine Fire

One of the great tasks of God's servants is to provide genuine God-fire, not humanly contrived emotional excitement. Enthusiasm and high energy are no substitute for the presence of God. John Witvliet said, "No one, no matter how charismatic, can make a moment holy by his or her own creativity, ingenuity, or effort."[2] We can nod our heads in agreement with that statement, but when our worship is dragging, what is our first inclination? Is it not to put a high-energy person on their feet, let a charismatic, passionate person get up front, or try to do something new and more creative? Our first cure for lifeless worship is often to get someone who has the capacity to light a fire under people, rather than seek the God who alone can light the fire in people. This is counterfeit fire—strange fire.

Samuel Chadwick recognized the existence of counterfeit fire when he said:

> Earth-fires can soon be set ablaze. It is so much easier to excite the passions than to kindle souls. Thorns crackle as they burn, and the flying sparks arrest and amuse. True, the fuel is soon exhausted and the fire fizzles out, but they serve while they last.[3]

Passion is a wonderful thing when it is the result of having the fire of God within. If it is generated by human energy or charisma, it is strange fire. Sadly, strange fires can sometimes be more appealing to the masses than the Ancient Fire.

Worship That Is Pretense

Hypocrisy brought the strongest of condemnations from the Lord. The worst offense to God is the pretense of spirituality. Jesus repeatedly condemned it in those who performed acts of worship but it was just a sham—a cover-up. He said, "These people honor me with their lips, but their hearts are far from me. They worship me in vain . . ." (Matt. 15:8–9). The condition of a worshiper's heart and the conduct of the worshiper's life must be consistent with the communication of that worshiper's lips. God cannot bless sin. The Scripture says: "The lamp of the wicked is snuffed out; the flame of his fire stops burning. The light in his tent becomes dark; the lamp beside him goes out" (Job 18:5–6). When there is sin in the worshiper's heart, what appears to be fire in the worship experience can be nothing more than strange fire.

Worship That Does Not Result in Changed Behavior

When people enter into the presence of God, they are confronted with His holiness and with their own lack of holiness. It happened with Isaiah when he saw the Lord, high and lifted up, and the angels singing of His holiness. Immediately he fell on his face and confessed his uncleanness, and God responded by cauterizing his uncleanness. Transformation is always the result of meeting with God. If our encounter with God is real, we must leave that encounter different than when we arrived. Our worship of God cannot be divorced from our behavior after worship. At least symbolically, could this be the meaning behind Ezekiel's words:

> When the people of the land come before the LORD at the appointed feasts, whoever enters by the north gate to worship is to go out the south gate; and whoever enters by the south gate is to go out the north gate. No one is to return through the gate by which he entered, but each is to go out the opposite gate. (Ezek. 46:9)

You can't leave the same way you came in, or what you have experienced is just strange fire.

Worship Preoccupied with the Novel

I don't want to be guilty of twisting Scripture in order to make a point, but the whole issue of Uzzah's death caused by mishandling the ark of the covenant raises several points, one of which has to do with deviation from God's prescribed practices to a new way of handling the ark. God was angry with Uzzah "because of his irreverent act" (2 Sam. 6:7), which was taking hold of the ark. A new cart had been brought in to transport the ark back to Jerusalem. This new cart was an unauthorized means of carrying the ark, which by God's command was to be carried by priests using poles placed through rings on each side of the ark. When the oxen pulling the cart stumbled, Uzzah instinctively took hold of the ark.

> One of the great tasks of God's servants is to provide genuine God-fire, not humanly contrived emotional excitement.

So using the new cart became the contributing cause of Uzzah's irreverent act.

Something is not bad simply because it is new. Creativity is a needed and desired quality in today's worship practices, but there are pitfalls to be avoided when bringing new practices into contemporary worship. There is a line between being creatively fresh and being irreverently novel that can be crossed.

> Christian history, particularly near the dawn of the early Church, offers many examples of people who took the gospel to their times in maverick ways. They weren't afraid to change methods or patterns of action. But they didn't try fresh approaches for the sake of newness; they discarded archaic ways because they no longer worked.[4]

The separation between divinely inspired creativity in worship and humanly contrived novelty is not great, but there is a line between them that should not be crossed. Because something is exciting and creative does not make it spiritual, any more than something is thought to be spiritual because it is old and tired. When the creative and the novel becomes the focus that brings excitement rather than God, it becomes strange fire.

> Transformation is always the result of meeting with God. If our encounter with God is real, we must leave that encounter different than when we arrived.

The question needs to be asked: How much creativity can you put into a sacrament and keep it a sacrament? I doubt that baptizing a person in a hot tub makes the baptism less spiritual than if it were done in a baptistery. However, I have been in services where a grape and a crouton, or pizza and soda have been substituted for bread and wine in the Lord's Supper. After all, we have learned to substitute common bread for unleavened bread and grape juice for fermented wine in most of our communion services. Is it the act, the attitude, or the elements of the Lord's Supper that make it sacred? The question of substituting elements should probably be, "Why?" Is it that bread and grape juice are not accessible, or that it is just more exciting and novel to use something else? When there is little separation in the mind of the partaker between the Lord's Table and the local pizza parlor, you have turned the sacrament of the Lord into strange fire.

Worship Focused On Something Other Than God

Nothing is to ever take the place of God in our worship. Jesus affirmed the single focus of our worship when He said, "For it is written: 'Worship the Lord your God, and serve him only'" (Matt. 4:10). We would protest the suggestion that we worship an idol—of any kind. We know idols to be carved images that pagans create that become visible substitutes for God. But whenever other things become substitutes for God in our worship, it becomes idolatry and is strange fire. Just because we come together on Sunday and call it a worship service does not mean we have acceptably worshiped God. We might feel better, either because we fulfilled our duty or had some need in our lives met, but was it more than strange fire? We might have experienced something exciting, but did emotional ecstasy become a substitute for the presence and power of God? It is possible for excitement to become our idol; or the easing of stress; or the need for fellowship; or the enjoyment of good music. Not everything that burns is fire from God, any more than everything that is buried is treasure.

The founder of the Salvation Army, William Booth, said:

> There are different kinds of fire; there is false fire . . . although we see here and there manifestations of what appears to us to be nothing more than mere earthly fire, we nonetheless prize and value, and seek for the genuine fire which comes from the altar of the Lord.[5]

Those who seek to worship God with all of their hearts intuitively know when they have really worshiped and when they have just gone through the motions. Strange fire never satisfies like the Ancient Fire.

Reflection

- What is the craziest thing you have experienced that happened in the name of worship?

- What creative thing have you tried that was intended to connect people with God but just didn't accomplish what you intended? Why was that so? What would you do differently?

- Are you open to think creatively about how you might enhance the worship experience of your people? How will you guard your creativity from becoming novelty?

Moving Forward

- Gather together a group of spiritually minded, creative persons who can help you plan each worship service. Encourage creative thinking that seeks to honor God and lift up Jesus, not to entertain or stir up less than spiritual emotion.

- Test your worship innovations with persons whose spiritual discernment you trust before doing them in public worship.

EIGHT

> "The burnt offering is to remain on the altar hearth *throughout the night*, till morning, and the fire must be kept burning on the altar . . . *Every morning* the priest is to add firewood and arrange the burnt offering on the fire and burn the fat of the fellowship offerings on it."
> —Lev. 6:9, 12-13, emphasis added

Add Fuel to the Fire

There is a daily-ness that accompanies worship. We cannot ignore God for six days and then expect to connect with Him in a dynamic way on Sunday. Worship leaders cannot enter into the worship service without adequate preparation. Experiencing the divine presence requires human preparation and participation. God brings the fire—we have to bring the firewood.

Once a fire has begun, it must be fed or it will die. Not only did I have to carry out the ashes from our old Warm Morning stove every evening, I had to carry in the coal. There was rhythm and ritual in keeping the fire burning: carry out the ashes, carry in the coal. Every evening and every morning there was something that needed to be done if the fire was to be kept burning.

The fire-tending responsibilities of the priests included adding firewood and arranging the offerings on the fire—every morning. If the fire was to be kept burning and the offerings on that fire were to be ready and appropriately arranged on the altar, a ritual of preparation and planning had to be in place. When the worship leaders woke in the morning things had to be ready, which meant thought had to be given to the task by the evening before and fuel for the fire had to be in place. Today's fire relies on yesterday's planning, and tomorrow's fire requires today's preparation.

Short-Term Planning

No worship leader should be caught by surprise when it comes to fulfilling God's requirements for preparation. Sunday comes the same time every week. There are always six days between Sundays—it is a ritual that never changes. What happens on Sunday requires planning and preparation that must be done throughout the preceding week. You expect the custodians of the building to have everything ready for use on Sunday morning, and responsible custodians of the fire must also spend time in thoughtful preparation and planning if everything related to worship is to be ready. This is contrary to the thought of some that the Holy Spirit works best when the only advance planning is the plan to be spontaneous. Paul told Timothy to preach the Word and be prepared to do it in season and out of season (2 Tim. 4:2); and to devote himself to reading, preaching, and teaching so people could see his progress (1 Tim. 4:13–16). Training, practice, and planning must accompany giftedness and responsibility.

> There is a daily-ness that accompanies worship. We cannot ignore God for six days and then expect to connect with Him in a dynamic way on Sunday.

Order of Worship

Contemporary worship planners may want to be more casual about having an order of worship than their predecessors, but everyone should have a plan for the worship service before going into it. There may be variation in the arrangements of the elements of worship, but most services will have a general plan. Like every other aspect of worship, some people find comfort and strength in a predictable order of worship, and others dislike anything that suggests predictability. The order of the worship elements may not be as important as the elements themselves.

Elements of Worship

Robert Webber says that worship renewal has moved toward a fourfold structure of: gathering together, hearing the Word, responding with thanksgiving, and being commissioned forth into the world.[1] Most worship planners will want to incorporate these general structural components into an order of worship that will include:

- Call to worship
- Invocation
- Singing
- Offering
- Scripture reading
- Sermon
- Call for response
- Benediction

The "every morning" preparations for Sunday worship should include communication and collaboration between the pastor and the other persons who will be participating in leading the service:

musicians; Scripture readers; and persons who will pray, make any announcements of ministry opportunities, give the call to worship, receive the offering, prepare the audio or video technology, and plan the drama or other aids to worship. Each element is a part of the whole and there should be a common thread that joins them together and communicates the importance of every person's contribution.

Short-term planning may go as far as timing the parts of the order of worship. In our fast-paced, short-attention span world, dead space, stalled moments, and extended unnecessary verbiage can kill a service. Leaders of worship should have a sense of the clock without calling attention to it. Better to have people leave wanting more than to have them feeling that the plane has circled the field several times and can't find a place to land.

"Every morning" planning allows for creative thought—making a connection between music, sermon, and drama; developing supporting video and PowerPoint; engaging more people in the service; focusing prayer more specifically; and communicating the purpose of the message and a corresponding spirit across the span of worship leaders.

Long-Term Planning

Short-term planning should be the final touches on the implementation of the long-term plan—the "throughout the night" planning. Without a long-term plan, the direction of the church will be disjointed and run in circles rather that move toward the objective of developing the spirituality of the people. The life of the church, including the objectives of each worship service and each sermon, should be governed by a master plan that moves people toward spiritual maturity and moves the church toward the fulfillment of its mission, locally and globally. If you have no target, you can shoot your arrow, draw some rings around it, and declare you have hit the target. Tragically, too many churches are hitting the targets they have drawn but are not hitting the ones that matter to God.

Sermon Preparation

Sermon preparation should be a long-term process as much as a short-term process. Each morning the preacher wakes with the knowledge Sunday is coming. Contrary to the practice of some, Saturday evening is not the most creative time for working on Sunday's message. In fact, it is a far better practice to begin the preparation for a sermon weeks before the time of its delivery. One of my mentors had the practice of using large envelopes to collect clippings and notes for sermons planned for the future. He would write the sermon title, subject, text, and projected date of delivery on the outside of the envelope. He kept a stack of these sermons-in-the-making envelopes on his desk in which he would collect items that would help develop the sermon. When it came time to give birth to the sermon, he would have collected a treasury of related material to draw upon in the final development of the message.

> The life of the church, including the objectives of each worship service and each sermon, should be governed by a master plan that moves people toward spiritual maturity and moves the church toward the fulfillment of its mission, locally and globally.

I tried his discipline but never fully mastered it. I resorted to spiral-bound notebooks in which I would collect sermon starters from my reading, experience with my people, and observations on life. A couple times a year I would get away from my office for a few days with my Bible, my notebooks, and a good book or two. I would spend the time praying for the mind of the Lord regarding the needs of my people and the direction I should go in my messages. Using the materials at hand, I would map out a suggested plan for several months in advance. Sermon ideas were organized in a tentative schedule, which could always be modified as I moved through the coming months. This planning changed the nature of the pressure of preparation I experienced each week. I was freer to think of the other elements of worship that could support the work God wanted to do through the message, the music, and the ministry to the people. I could communicate the direction of sermon themes weeks in advance, which allowed those in charge of music and other elements of the services to be creative and prepared to offer their best in leading the worship experience.

Christian (Church) Year

Those who follow the lectionary allow others to map out for them where they will go with Scripture readings as well as sermon texts and topics. Non-liturgical churches may feel too constrained by the structures of the lectionary but can discover that following the general seasons of the Christian year will provide a wonderful format for long-term worship planning.

Jewish worship was built around seven prominent feasts or festivals. The Law of Moses said, "These are the LORD's appointed feasts, the sacred assemblies you are to proclaim at their appointed times . . ." (Lev. 23:4). These feasts were: Passover, Unleavened Bread, Firstfruits, Pentecost, Trumpets, Day of Atonement, and Tabernacles. These feasts, in their appointed times, were the pattern that guided them through the year, reminding them of the significant events of their spiritual history when God acted on their behalf.

The early church also developed a pattern to guide its worship through the year, reminding its people of the life and redemptive work of Christ. The Jewish celebrations largely focused on their exodus from Egypt, while the Christian church year focuses on the life and ministry of Christ. This pattern is referred to as the liturgical year, the Christian year, or the Church year.

> The Christian calendar is organized around two major centers of Sacred Time: Advent, Christmas, and Epiphany; and Lent, Holy Week, and Easter, concluding at Pentecost. The rest of the year following Pentecost is known as Ordinary Time, from the word "ordinal," which simply means counted time (First Sunday after Pentecost, etc.). Ordinary Time is used to focus on various aspects of the Faith, especially the mission of the church in the world. Some church traditions break up ordinary time into a Pentecost Season, (Pentecost until the next to last Sunday of August) and Kingdomtide (last Sunday of August until the beginning of Advent).[2]

Most pastors who seek to have a long-term plan for church life will adopt a modified Christian church year that will include:

- Advent—begins the fourth Sunday before Christmas and ends Christmas Eve
- Lent—forty weekdays (not counting Sundays) beginning with Ash Wednesday and ending with Easter
- Holy week—the last week of lent leading up to Easter (includes Palm Sunday, Maundy Thursday, and Good Friday)
- Easter—the first Sunday following the first full moon after the spring equinox
- Pentecost—the seventh Sunday after Easter

Modern additions have been made to the church year, such as Reformation Sunday and Thanksgiving. It is interesting that non-liturgical churches may choose to disregard the prescriptive nature of following the church year, but would never think of skipping Mother's Day, Father's Day, or Thanksgiving. It should be unthinkable in our theological tradition to allow Pentecost Sunday to slide by without even a tipping of the hat.

Planned and purposeful observance of the Christian seasons and festivals can become an important tool for education and discipleship in the faith, as well as a vehicle for spiritual growth and vitality.[3] The church year allows the church to have a balanced approach to its worship life. It avoids the tendency for worship leaders to become sidetracked into less significant events while leaving out the major tenets of the church's faith.[4]

There are thriving churches in our tradition that have chosen to follow this modified church year, which means they observe the liturgical seasons without following the lectionary. One such church is College Wesleyan Church in Marion, Indiana. The church is contiguous to Indiana Wesleyan University and ministers to both community and campus. It has been in existence for more than 125 years, and is thriving today under the leadership of Dr. Steven DeNeff.

It was this church's announcement of an Ash Wednesday service that caught my attention. Not simply because it indicated that it would include the application of ash to the forehead and the induction of absolution to worshipers (this would be expected at many liturgical churches on Ash Wednesday), but because the announcement came from a church that is a part of a non-liturgical tradition and has many young adults in its constituency. I contacted the senior pastor and made an appointment to spend some time with him and his worship leader to talk about this service, as well as other attempts to capture the meaning behind some of the original worship rituals of the church that have largely been left behind as practices that no longer carry the Fire.

The pastor said they were following the Christian year as a guide to their worship because it helped them to develop a balanced approach to preaching, teaching, and worship. It gave direction and focus that kept hobbies from taking center stage and difficult subjects from being addressed. They preceded occasions such as Ash Wednesday with teaching that would inform participants in the meaning behind the worship activity. It was an intentional effort to expand the experience of the people to appreciate historic ritual, expressed in fresh ways, in order to facilitate their spiritual growth and development.

The season of Lent at College Church was built around a special sermon and worship series that focused on the cross of Christ and culminated in "calling people to the cross." A large rugged cross was prominent at the front of the sanctuary, positioned in different places for the different emphases of each Sunday. On Easter Sunday, the cross was positioned in the front center of the sanctuary with an impressive life-sized painting of the crucified Christ hanging on it. (It had been painted by a member of the congregation especially for this Sunday.) At the close of the service, individuals who had anything in their life they wanted to bring to the cross for the crucified-now-risen Christ to remove from them, was invited to come forward, stand before the cross for as long as they wanted. The response of the people became one of those special times of divine visitation. A steady stream of people, lasting over thirty minutes, brought themselves and their needs to the cross. Some touched the figure of the Savior, weeping as they confessed their need of Him. Couples stood with their arms around each other, embraced by the grace of God that accompanied the verbal and visual presentation of new life available in Christ.

Blossoming of the Cross

At the last church I pastored, we established a meaningful ritual for observing the Lenten season. We placed a large, rather rugged cross at the front of our worship center and referenced it throughout the Sundays of Lent in messages that centered on the cross. During one of the messages based on Colossians 2:13–14, "He forgave us all our sins, having canceled the written code, with its regulations, that was against us and that stood opposed to us; he took it away, nailing it to the cross," I took a scroll that represented our sins and drove a nail through it into the cross. Worshipers were invited to write something on a piece of paper that represented their need for forgiveness and place it in a container at the foot of the cross. These papers were then burned as an offering to the only One who has the power to forgive. On Easter Sunday, worshipers were encouraged to bring spring flowers from their yards and gardens to "blossom the cross." Cut flowers were on hand for those who came without flowers, and every person was asked to come to the front of the church and place their flower in florist netting and greenery that now covered the cross that was draped with white cloth. When everyone had brought their floral offering, the once rugged cross was covered with beautiful flowers. It provided a teaching moment about the redemptive work of Christ which takes the ugliness of our lives and, through the sacrifice made on the cross, brings life and beauty. It became a ritual of our church that was anticipated annually because it was rich with meaning.

> Planned and purposeful observance of the Christian seasons and festivals can become an important tool for education and discipleship in the faith, as well as a vehicle for spiritual growth and vitality.

There is meaning and spiritual value in some of the time-honored ways of doing things in worship that can be captured in new, creative, and contemporary expressions that will enhance our worship experiences. In order to do this, pastors need to:

- pay the price necessary to do advance preparation;
- assemble a group of creative, spiritually minded people who can help plan worship;
- map out a direction for his or her worship and sermons that will lead the people into spiritual maturity;
- become acquainted with the Church year and how others are celebrating it; and
- study some of the ritual practiced by the church over the centuries to see how it can be utilized in new ways.

Reflection

- What have you done today to prepare yourself for worship next Sunday?

- When have you missed a great opportunity to enrich your worship service because you did not plan far enough in advance so you could allow God to stimulate your thinking, gather the necessary resources, or ask the right people to participate? How can you avoid missing such an opportunity next time around?

Moving Forward

- Begin an annual worship planning calendar. Include the emphases of the Christian year, civil holidays, and the themes of disciple-making that will assist the spiritual development and maturity of your people.

- Begin a preaching planning schedule that will be integrated with your worship planning calendar. This is spiritual work, so get away where you can focus and bathe the process in prayer.

- Enlist people to help you develop the worship activities that will make the most of the emphases on your calendar.

NINE

> "The fire and wood are here . . . but *where is the lamb* for the burnt offering?"
> —Gen. 22:7, emphasis added

Remember the Lamb

You would not think of planning or attending a birthday party and then completely ignoring the person whose birthday made the celebration possible. Without that person, the party has no purpose, except to make the party rather than the person the reason for meeting, which would be an affront to the person. We miss the whole point of worship when our coming together becomes more important to us than celebrating the presence of the One who invites us to come to Him.

The Day of Worship

No ritual of the Christian church is more widely practiced than meeting for worship on Sunday. Christian worship is intended to focus on Jesus and His redemptive intervention in the life of sinful humanity.

Early Christians shifted the day of worship from the last day of the week, the Jewish Sabbath, to the first day of the week, our Sunday. This shift took place as a means of celebrating the resurrection of Jesus Christ which came on the first day of the week. Rather than simply resting from labor, Christians join together to celebrate the life of Jesus as a means of spiritual renewal and empowerment for a new week of labor. Jesus is the whole reason for meeting. As much as we might enjoy each other's company, coming together for the party is not the purpose—focusing on the person Jesus is the purpose.

> We miss the whole point of worship when our coming together becomes more important to us than celebrating the presence of the One who invites us to come to Him.

The Lamb of God

There is more than contrived drama going on in the biblical record of Abraham's act of obedience to God when he prepared to offer his son as a sacrifice.

> Abraham took the wood for the burnt offering and placed it on his son Isaac, and he himself carried the fire and the knife. As the two of them went on together, Isaac spoke up and said to his father Abraham, "Father?"
>
> "Yes, my son?" Abraham replied.
>
> "The fire and wood are here," Isaac said, "but where is the lamb for the burnt offering?"
>
> Abraham answered, "God himself will provide the lamb for the burnt offering, my son." And the two of them went on together. (Gen. 22:6–8)

Abraham made all of the preparations for his sacrifice. He had wood for the burnt offering. He carried fire to ignite the wood. He brought along a knife with which to take the life of the living creature that would be offered to God. He was fully prepared to worship God and to do the unthinkable—to offer his beloved son Isaac as the sacrifice. Then Isaac, who understood the practices of worship, recognized something was missing. The act of sacrificial worship would not be complete without a lamb, so he asked a most perceptive question: "Where is the lamb?" (v. 7). Abraham's response to Isaac's question is a hint of things to come. There is something here that transcends the moment and looks hundreds of years into the future when God would provide the Lamb that would take away the sins of the world and make the Jewish sacrificial system no longer necessary (or acceptable). Jesus is the Lamb that makes connection with God possible. He is the only access available to us by which we can approach God in worship. Jesus said, "No one comes to the Father except through me" (John 14:6). Everything else may be in place and everyone else may be present, but if the Lamb is not there, worship cannot take place.

If it is Christian worship, it must be Christo-centric. Regardless of our preferred style of worship, if Jesus is not present, recognized, and honored, our worship experience is no more than a secular performance designed for our own enjoyment. If there is no Lamb, there is no acceptable worship, and there can be no Fire.

> Regardless of our preferred style of worship, if Jesus is not present, recognized, and honored, our worship experience is no more than a secular performance designed for our enjoyment. If there is no Lamb, there is no acceptable worship, and there can be no Fire.

No Other Name

Sadly, I have attended Christian worship services in which the name of Jesus was never mentioned—not in the lyrics of the music or in the words of the message. It might be argued that whenever two or three are gathered together with the purpose of connecting with God, He is there. It might be assumed that we don't have to acknowledge His presence; He is there whether we mention His name or not. I don't agree with that sentiment. First of all, the promise of His presence is given to those who meet "in Jesus' name." How can you meet in His name if His name is never mentioned and He is never acknowledged? It is through His name that we access redemption and are given the privilege of entering into the presence of a holy God.

Jesus said if He is lifted up in witness and worship, He would draw people to himself. If the Lamb is absent, the emphasis on sin and the need for a redeemer is minimized. There is too much therapeutic gospel being presented today that promises help for your hurts and improvement of your situation—but not salvation from your sins. The message is that you need God to feel better, but not to be made better. The Lamb is not needed if there is no sin that needs forgiveness. And, there is no forgiveness if the Lamb is not offered as a remedy for those who have sin from which they need deliverance.

It is possible to talk of Jesus as our friend and as a good teacher whose companionship and words make life better for us. But if you are talking seriously about Jesus, you must proclaim Him as Savior, which requires you to address the sin problem in the human heart. Acknowledging the Lamb requires acknowledgement of our need for a redeemer.

We must recover a focus on the Lamb in the ritual of the church. We meet on His day, in His Name, and in His house. So where is the Lamb? How do we acknowledge Him?

Tell Me the Story of Jesus

Heaven will be filled with singing the praise of the Lamb who was slain from the foundations of the world. He will occupy the lyrics of whatever style of music is sung in heaven—which I imagine will either be a little bit of every style we have here, or something so far superior that we will wonder why God ever allowed us to sing the way we did. I tend to think the important thing will not be the type or style of the music, but the lyrics that matter. And it is the lyrics of the music that I think is important about today's church music.

Music

If Christ is mentioned and honored, then there may be some redemptive value in any type of music. If He is absent or dishonored, then there is no style of music that belongs in Christian worship. It is probably unfair to make generalizations that cannot be substantiated, but it is my personal observation that the present trend in music used in most contemporary worship services tends not to be Christ-centered.

Beyond being a means of focusing on Christ, the ritual of singing has been a primary means of communicating doctrinal truth through the centuries of the church's existence. Music in worship is more than an attempt to satisfy an inner desire to move to a beat, but rather to vocalize our praise of God and to transmit His redemptive truth from one generation to another. Again, it is my judgment that a steady diet of praise choruses, that neither lift up the name of Jesus nor proclaim the historic faith, will result in a spiritually immature and faith-starved generation. Contemporary gospel music should not be left out of our worship, but we should certainly screen the appropriateness of what we sing and periodically do an audit of what we have sung to see that the Lamb is included and our theology has been clearly affirmed by the lyrics.

Sermon

Proclamation of the gospel has always been at the center of Christian worship. Following the reformation, many worship centers included a pulpit, elevated from the platform, from which the Word of God was read and proclaimed. The elevated pulpit symbolized the primacy of the sermon and accented the authority of the word spoken from there. In most non-liturgical churches, the pulpit was brought down to the platform level while pastors sought to narrow the gap between pulpit and pew. More recently, the pulpit has disappeared to make room for a communication style that is more intimate and less inhibiting. Along with the pulpit, the communion table has disappeared too, which previously was a means of visually proclaiming the centrality of Christ and His atonement.

Preaching style has largely changed along with the architectural changes. The prevailing preaching style is more conversational and delivery is often made without notes. The content of the sermon is certainly more important than the style of delivery or whether or not there is a pulpit. We just need to be sure we don't throw Jesus out along with the pulpit and communion table.

> Acknowledging the Lamb requires acknowledgment of our need for a redeemer.

Paul spoke of the simplicity and power of the gospel he preached: ". . . we preach Christ crucified" (1 Cor. 1:23). The good news of the gospel is that Jesus Christ has provided the means by which we can be saved from our sin. It is not a prosperity gospel, or a therapeutic gospel, or a self-help gospel—this is good news that there is a remedy in Christ for the root cause of humanity's problem, which is sin. The ritual that keeps the fire burning is the preaching of Christ crucified—the Lamb that was slain.

The need for effective preaching has not changed. The authority of the Word of God has not changed. The power of the gospel to transform lives has not changed. The magnetic draw of Jesus has not changed. Changes to the ritual of proclaiming the gospel of Jesus Christ are inevitable, but changes from proclaiming the gospel should not occur. Too often in contemporary settings, it is the music that is considered to be the worship time, and the sermon is simply thrown in because that is the way it has always been done. The sermon is a place to lift up the Lamb of God who takes away the sins of the world and let Him draw people into His saving embrace. Preach Jesus and you will never lack for an audience—both God and sinners will show up for the meeting.

> The sermon is a place to lift up the Lamb of God who takes away the sins of the world and let Him draw people into His saving embrace.

The Lord's Supper

It is necessary that we intentionally include Christ in the language used in our songs and sermons. Another major focus on Jesus as Savior should occur through our ritual of observing the Lord's Supper. This sacrament has always occupied a prominent place in most Christian traditions, but has increased in its importance in contemporary worship. Contemporary worshipers want a fuller engagement of themselves in the contemporary worship experience. People in our congregations are a part of a culture of experience.[1] This is not simply a scientific age where people are satisfied with facts alone. Reality for them needs to be more tangible and experiential. Experiences are events that engage individuals in a personal way and become memorable for them. The more senses that can be involved, the richer and more memorable the experience becomes. The Lord's Supper or Communion or the Eucharist is a ritual that engages hearing, sight, touch, and taste. It appeals to mind, body, and spirit. It is valued as a sacrament in which grace is communicated to us and as an experience in which we tangibly connect with Christ through the means He rather graphically instructed His disciples to do (John 6:53–57).

There are those who celebrate Communion but on a limited basis. Their reasoning often is that doing it on a regular basis causes a loss of its specialness, and in the frequent repetition, the sacrament becomes dead ritual. They should try telling that to their stomach the next time they feel hungry, or to their spouse when they decide to make "I love you" more special by only saying it once every three months. Communion is a meal of intimacy with Christ and with the other communicants that should not be relegated to insignificance through infrequent participation. If we neglect it, we become spiritually malnourished. As Keith Drury says:

> John Wesley fought the lackadaisical attitude toward the Lord's Supper in his day, and we must fight it today. We think communion "takes too long" or "isn't relevant to daily life" or "it is a downer and we want brighter services." So we assign it to some sideshow service that most people can skip. Shame on us! No wonder the church lacks holiness—it lacks one of the chief means of grace, the Lord's Supper.[2]

In his sermon titled "The Means of Grace," Wesley recognized the Lord's Supper to be a *means of grace*, which he in turn described as "outward signs, words, or actions, ordained of God, and appointed for this end, to be the ordinary channels whereby he might convey to men, preventing, justifying, or sanctifying grace."[3] Wesley said, "As our bodies are strengthened by bread and wine, so are our souls by these tokens of the body and the blood of Christ. This is the food of our souls: This gives strength to perform our duty, and leads us on to perfection."[4] Too often we may overlook Paul's word in 1 Corinthians 11:30, in which he said that the neglect of the Lord's Supper caused many to be weak and sick!

Great debates and serious disputes have been generated over the centuries as people have tried to understand the nature of this sacrament and its value to the believer. Wesleyan tradition has come to view the Lord's Supper in a variety of ways, all of which find substance in the Scriptures. A collective reading of the several passages in which the Lord's Supper is mentioned projects at least five different images upon this meal, that of: (1) thanksgiving to the Father, (2) commemoration of Christ, (3) sacrifice of ourselves, (4) fellowship of the faithful, and (5) a foretaste of the kingdom. Leaders of worship do well to vary the emphasis from Communion service to Communion service, which in turn varies the mood from solemn introspection to joyful celebration—from a private table for two to a communal "we, who are many, are one body, for we all partake of the one loaf" (1 Cor. 10:17).

Jesus used the time of the Passover feast to prepare His disciples for His imminent crucifixion and shared with them what we call the Lord's Supper. At that time, He asked if the disciples would remember Him. He then shared with them the simple meal representing His broken body and shed blood. As He did this He said, "Do this in remembrance of me" (Luke 22:19). The apostle Paul added: "For whenever you eat this bread and drink this cup, you proclaim the Lord's death" (1 Cor. 11:26). But while giving them tokens of His death, Jesus asked them to eat and to remember *Him*—not just the cruelty of crucifixion, but His life, His teaching, His loving, His caring ministry.

And a few days later, after His resurrection, Jesus had a meal at Emmaus with some disciples, who even after walking some distance with Him, did not recognize Him. As they sat together, He asked the question, "Don't you understand? Don't you know me?" And He opened the Scriptures and broke bread with them. It was in the breaking of bread that their eyes were opened, they knew Him, and they came to new understanding about Him and His mission (Luke 24:13–35).

Then, within that same time frame, Jesus came to Peter and some others, who in their frustration and loss following the crucifixion, were fishing but with no success. Jesus told them where the fish were and then invited them to shore to eat a meal He had prepared. It was in this setting that Jesus looked Peter in the eye—Peter who swore that he didn't even know Jesus and wasn't a follower of Him—and asked: "Simon [Peter] . . . do you love me?" (John 21).

There were four questions Jesus asked while sharing meals of revelation and relationship with His disciples: Do you love me? Do you know me? Do you understand? Will you remember me? I like to think that when I come to Communion, I am at such a meal with Jesus—a time in which

> Communion is a meal of intimacy with Christ and with the other communicants that should not be relegated to insignificance through infrequent participation.

I experience a combination of all three—a meal of remembering, a meal of revelation, and a meal of relationship. The Lord's Supper is so rich with meaning and spiritual vitality, why would any worship leader withhold the opportunity to partake of it with regularity?

In the name of being "contemporary," the ritual of the Lord's Supper is often reduced to the act of eating and drinking, with little or no preparation of persons for the sacred act, or the offering of prayer for the consecration of the elements. The Lord's Supper is not a meaningless ritual to be tacked on to the end of a service and hurried through so people can beat others to the local restaurant and get some real food. Worshipers should be offered the real food of the soul without being rushed. There should be adequate preparation for the meal, which includes prayer that God would take the common elements of bread and grape juice and consecrate them to spiritual good in the souls of those who partake.

Guard the Sacred

While attending an out-of-town conference, I visited a large, popular church because I wanted to hear the pastor. The worship folder that was handed to me let me know that the Lord's Supper would be observed during the service. I was glad, since I always look forward to partaking of this most holy sacrament. What I did not realize was that this was also Super Bowl Sunday and that city's team was playing in the game. The entire service was overtaken by the euphoria of this high day in the sporting calendar.

> It is an awesome thing to handle the body and the blood of Christ and to offer it to spiritually hungry people.

Prior to communion, a lay person offered a prayer, and as he concluded his prayer he said, "And Lord, help our team win tonight." The congregation exploded with cheers and applause. We then partook of the communion elements. I participated, but somewhere between the prayer and the bread, the sacredness of the moment was lost. The broken body and shed blood of Christ took a back seat to the Super Bowl.

It is an awesome thing to handle the body and the blood of Christ and to offer it to spiritually hungry people. Few things fulfill my sense of calling more than to look a worshiper in the eye, offer them the bread and cup, and say to them, "The body of our Lord Jesus Christ broken for you . . . The blood of our Lord Jesus Christ shed for you . . ." There is power in the sacrament. There is an opportunity for pastor and people to connect in a way and at a level that nothing else can provide.

Without the Lamb there can be no access to the Father. Without the Lamb there is no ability to worship. The Ancient Fire shows up wherever the Lamb is accepted and honored.

Reflection

- In what specific ways was the need for Jesus focused on in your last worship service? Where did you have an opportunity to point people to the forgiving, cleansing, healing, life-transforming work of Jesus?

- Does your selection of music include a clear lifting up of Jesus as the answer to sinful humanity's greatest need?

- How often do you preach about the many benefits of the atonement that are available only through faith in Jesus Christ, as opposed to appeals to and helps for living a better life and doing better things?

Moving Forward

- Keep a record of the songs you use in worship. After a period of time, do an audit and identify the messages communicated through the lyrics of the songs.

- Seek an appropriate balance in the style and lyrics of your music to include celebration, reflection, praise, worship, faith themes, and proclamation of salvation in Christ.

- Schedule frequent times for observing the Lord's Supper, emphasizing the messages that rise out of the act.

- Vary the mode and means of serving communion (i.e.: intinction or individual cups; coming forward to the altar or served at their place of seating; common loaf or wafer).

> "I [John] baptize you with water. But . . . He [Jesus] will baptize you with the Holy Spirit and with fire." —Luke 3:16

Baptized By Water and Fire

Fire and water don't mix—except when it comes to baptism. The One who baptizes by fire was himself baptized with water, and we are urged to experience both baptisms.

Water baptism is a sacrament through which God communicates His grace and by which the persons baptized connect with the presence and power of God. Water baptism is not a substitute for baptism with the Holy Spirit, but water baptism can be a means of experiencing the fire of God's Spirit. Most evangelical churches recognize baptism and the Lord's Supper as sacraments—outward signs of an inward grace.[1] Sacraments are rituals either initiated by Christ or authorized by His participation in them and are means through which God connects with His people.

When I was a youngster, I accompanied a group of people from the church my dad pastored to a rather secluded place along the banks of a small creek a few miles out of town, to baptize some new Christians. This was before we had the more sanitized baptisteries where new believers could be discretely baptized away from the prying eyes of curious onlookers. One of the converts to be baptized had come to faith in Christ after a number of years of open sin and was farther along in adulthood than is often the case with new Christians. I imagined he was the inspiration for the first line of the old hymn: "Years I spent in vanity and pride." This was a very emotional experience for him and he emerged joyfully from his dunking in the creek. What helped cement this moment in my young mind was that during numerous prayer meeting testimony times after that, I would hear him recount the day he "saw [his] sins floating down Turkey Creek."

One of our church leaders returned from visiting new churches in India. While there he visited a very nice, newly constructed church where a thriving congregation regularly saw people from the Hindu community convert to Christianity. He said that after visiting the church, he expressed his surprise to the pastor that the new facility did not include a baptistery. The pastor expressed equal surprise that he was asked the question. He indicated that new converts in his church were paraded to the community fountain in the center of the marketplace where they were baptized in full view of everyone so they would know the converts had experienced a new spiritual birth. He said it helped create seriously committed believers.

> Water baptism is a sacrament through which God communicates His grace and by which the persons baptized connect with the presence and power of God.

Adult Baptism

Adult (believer's) baptism is a ritual that is rich with meaning. It is a sign of a covenant between God and the believer. It is a means of grace. It is an initiatory act which declares the person baptized to be a part of the larger Christian community. It is an open testimony of the believer's faith and of the cleansing work of Christ, celebrated by the church and witnessed by the world. It is an act of obedience to the command of Christ and a participation in the fulfillment of the Great Commission to "make disciples of all nations, baptizing them in the name of the Father and of the Son and of the Holy Spirit" (Matt. 28:19). It is an act of humility as the candidate submits to the authority and care of God's representative who officiates over the baptism.

> The early church often withheld baptism from new converts until after extensive preparation in matters of doctrine and practice.

It is a voluntary physical act done in concert with a deep spiritual desire to be a disciple of Christ and to be discipled in the faith. It is symbolic of the washing away of sin; of death to the old life; and of rising to new life (Rom. 6:4). There is deep meaning in the ritual.

Baptism is serious business with a celebrative outcome. It is both solemn and festive—but never trivialized by thoughtless and frivolous handling of the rite. The early church often withheld baptism from new converts until after extensive preparation in matters of doctrine and practice. Usually Lent, the days leading up to Easter, was a time for doctrinal study, fasting, and spiritual reflection that ended with baptism on Easter Sunday, a practice being reintroduced in many contemporary churches. What an exciting way to celebrate new life in the resurrected and resurrecting Savior.

New Hope Church

One of these contemporary churches is New Hope Church located in the heart of Tar Heel country near Raleigh, North Carolina. The church was planted in 2002, by Benji Kelley who graduated from Duke Divinity School before completing the Beeson doctoral program at Asbury Theological Seminary. Benji felt compelled to plant a church in the area he came to love while doing his graduate work, so he started the church with his wife and two children. I visited his church seven years later on the second Sunday in their newly constructed church facility. Over two thousand people packed the two worship services on the opening Sunday and it was estimated that over fifty cars were turned away because there was no space left in the parking lot.

But, there is a significant difference between drawing a crowd and drawing people to Christ. I had great confidence in Benji, but I wanted to experience for myself what was happening at New Hope. What I witnessed was a contemporary church that had not forsaken the substance of meaningful worship in a traditional sense—in fact they purposefully have instituted historic worship ritual in contemporary expressions. Their baptismal services may not be conducted at the center of the marketplace as our church in India, but New Hope places great value in the sacrament of baptism. In the center of a large courtyard outside of the entrance to their ministry center is an attractive fountain and pool. It is here that new converts testify to their faith through baptism—out in full view of the community. Fifty new believers were baptized there following the first Easter Sunday morning worship service in the new ministry center.

College Wesleyan Church

Another thriving church is College Wesleyan Church in Marion, Indiana, contiguous to Indiana Wesleyan University. As stated earlier, the church ministers to both community and campus, which provides for a rich mixture of ages, cultures, and generations. The church recently occupied new facilities that were purposely designed to express the church's theology. One of the main features is obvious as soon as you open the main doors of the building and enter the large atrium foyer with its towering high ceiling. The far wall is rough stone with water running down the face of the wall into a baptismal pool. The atrium becomes the gathering place for the congregation when candidates are baptized. The atrium also has a place in its center, under the spire-like cross that extends out of the roof above, that serves as a baptismal font for infants. The baptism of new converts, by physical construction and actual practice, is at the center of church life.

> The baptism of infants is a testimony of the faith of the parents and a belief in the merits of the atonement being sufficient for persons unable by age or mental impairment to make moral and spiritual choices.

Christian baptism is a ritual where both fire and water mix. Nothing energizes a congregation as much as witnessing the fulfillment of the Great Commission as people respond to the preaching and teaching of the gospel, become disciples, and receive the sacrament of baptism. Jesus was baptized and suddenly the Trinity—Father, Son, and Holy Spirit—were present (Matt. 3:13–17). The same happens every time a new believer is baptized.

Infant Baptism

There tends to be a sharp divide, not just between theological traditions but sometimes even within them regarding infant baptism. There are those who encourage parents to have their infants baptized and those who discourage or even forbid the practice. My denomination makes this statement:

> Since children are born into this world with natures inclined to sin, and yet the prevenient grace of God provides for their redemption during the period before reaching the age of accountability, those parents who so choose may testify to their faith in God's provision by presenting their small children for baptism, while those who prefer to emphasize baptism as a testimony by individual believers to their own act of faith may present their children for dedication.²

The baptism of infants is a testimony of the faith of the parents and a belief in the merits of the atonement being sufficient for persons unable by age or mental impairment to make moral and spiritual choices. This assurance is grounded in an understanding of prevenient grace, or preventing grace as Wesley sometimes called it.

Lyle Williams, in an unpublished study paper presented at a Consultation on Church Doctrines in 1974, said:

> Even John Calvin, representing one major branch of Protestantism, insisted that the gracious promises of the New Covenant included the children of the church. He said: "Since the Lord, immediately after the covenant was made with Abraham, ordered it to be sealed in infants by an outward sacrament, how can it be said that Christians are not to attest it in the present day, and seal it in their children?" Wesley, whose Arminianism has made Arminius known among modern evangelicals, agrees with Calvin and says: "As circumcision was then the way of entering into this covenant, so baptism is now."³

There are those who argue that infants are incapable of doing anything to affect their salvation. Whatever position we may take on the matter, we dare not construe that argument to infer that adults can do something to affect their salvation. Salvation is all of grace—to which we respond in faith to receive. Infants can not yet exercise faith for saving faith, but infant baptism is a declaration that the prevenient grace of God saves the child, and the parents covenant with God that the grace that presently covers the child will be nourished through their care and will, as much as they can assist, become the personal declaration of faith when the child is capable.

The baptism of an infant is a wonderful ritual by which to teach the church about grace, about parental responsibility, and about the powerful influence that is released within the church when they wrap their arms around children and declare them to be in the family of God. Congregations should take seriously their pledge to do everything they can to see that no child is left behind or allowed to ever slip away.

Affirmation by Adults

Persons who were baptized as infants often want to affirm as adults what their parents did on their behalf. Being re-baptized is not a requirement and should, within reason, be discouraged. If baptism is an initiatory rite of the church, a person does not need multiple initiatory events. The covenant entered into between God and the infant, appropriately represented by the parents, need not be reestablished. In order for adults baptized as infants to personally participate in the sacrament of baptism, my denomination has provided a ritual which allows them to declare their faith in Christ and affirm their baptism.[4] This ritual has been very meaningful for persons who appreciate the faith of their parents but feel they need to do something personally regarding their baptism.

Dedication of Children

Many in the Wesleyan/Holiness tradition, perhaps influenced more by Baptist thinking than their own Methodist roots, do not practice infant baptism but rather desire to dedicate their children to God. This follows the Jewish custom of presenting children to God shortly after their birth, which was observed by Joseph and Mary on behalf of Jesus (Luke 2:22). This ritual is far more than showing off a newborn. It is a time to recognize the responsibilities of being a parent and to recognize that a child is a special gift from God with a purpose to be fulfilled for the glory of God. Preparing parents for the act of dedication can become rich soil in which to plant the seeds of salvation, for even unsaved parents often want to do right by their newborn children and see that they receive the benefits of life in the church. It is one of those great teachable moments in parents' lives when they are particularly open to spiritual things. God loves little ones, and He loves to use them to get to parents who need to be introduced to Him.

As a pastor, I officiated at far more infant dedications than baptisms. Both can be significant events for parents, families, and congregations. The ritual for both dedication and baptism acknowledges the responsibility of both parents and congregation, and the need for help from God.

If we believe baptism to be a means of grace, then grace accompanies the sacrament whether experienced by adult or by infant. I was dedicated as an infant, not baptized. I distinctly remember when, as a young teenager, I was snooping in my parent's closet just before Christmas to see if I could get a sneak peak at any presents that might be hidden there. I opened a box and there discovered a certificate

> The baptism of an infant is a wonderful ritual by which to teach the church about grace, about parental responsibility, and about the powerful influence that is released within the church when they wrap their arms around children and declare them to be in the family of God.

declaring my dedication to God. I had not drifted from the faith I had placed in Christ at nine years of age, but a kind of casualness about spiritual things had crept in. As I read the certificate that testified to this act by my parents in which they declared me to belong to God, I determined I would never violate the dedication done on my behalf. I belonged to God, not just to my parents—and especially not just to myself. What my parents did for me mattered, even years later. Grace is a wonderful thing.

Baptism By the Spirit

Jesus encouraged water baptism but also opened the way for and pointed us toward a second, more important baptism by fire. He completed the work of the atonement and then the Holy Spirit was released in a fuller way to implement all of the benefits of that atonement. It is the Holy Spirit who enables effective holy living and energizes effective worship. Whether we declare ourselves to be liturgical or non-liturgical makes no difference if the Holy Spirit is not actively engaging our spirits as we worship, enhancing our praise, convicting us of sin and truth, interceding in our behalf, interpreting the Divine will to us, and enabling our service to a broken world.

> Whether we declare ourselves to be liturgical or non-liturgical makes no difference if the Holy Spirit is not actively engaging our spirits as we worship, enhancing our praise, convicting us of sin and truth, interceding in our behalf, interpreting the Divine will to us, and enabling our service to a broken world.

The Holy Spirit and the life He generates cannot be contained in rigid, restrictive structures of our making. Pastors have the privilege and responsibility of leading their congregations in experiencing the stimulating, uplifting, empowering presence of the Holy Spirit on a regular basis through the various activities of the church community. Too often, the wine of Holy Spirit activity has been programmed to fit into inflexible wineskins, which causes the wine to be lost and the wineskins to be discarded. It is also possible to force the Holy Spirit into new wineskins that are unfit for His filling, and without the affirming presence and power of the Ancient Fire, they are ineffective.

Sadly, the dynamic of the Holy Spirit's presence in the community life of the church can be lost for the lack of appropriate wineskins. The forms, rituals, liturgies, and sacraments intended to convey the presence and power of God can become inflexible, lose touch with life, and lose their meaning. Doing things in new ways is not necessarily the answer. The Spirit may not choose to work through novel devices that do not carry the meaning originally intended. Samuel Chadwick has written:

> The Church is powerless without the Fire of the Holy Ghost . . . The one vital need is Fire. How we may receive it, where we may find it, by what means we may retain it, are the most vital and urgent questions of our time. One thing we know: it comes only with the presence of the Spirit of God, Himself the Spirit of Fire. God alone can send the Fire. It is His Pentecostal gift.[5]

Samuel Chadwick was born in the industrial north of England in 1860. He came to realize early in his ministry that he was largely being ineffective. Staring defeat in the face and sensing his lack of real power, an intense hunger was kindled within him for more of God. At this point, he heard the testimony of someone who had been baptized by an experience of the Holy Spirit. So, with a few friends he covenanted to pray and search the Scriptures until God sent revival.

One evening, he was praying over his next sermon when a powerful sense of conviction settled on him. His pride, blindness, and reliance on human methods paraded before his eyes as God humbled him. Well into the night he wrestled and repented, then he gathered his sermons together and set fire to them! Almost immediately the Holy Spirit fell upon him.

> I could not explain what had happened, but it was a bigger thing than I had ever known. There came into my soul a deep peace, a thrilling joy, and a new sense of power. My mind was quickened. I felt I had received a new faculty of understanding. Every power was baptized. My body was quickened. There was a new sense of spring and vitality, a new power of endurance and a strong man's exhilaration in big things.[6]

If we could package that up, we could market some really big conferences and sell a lot of three-ring binders. Isn't the result of which Chadwick testifies the desire of every minister who wants to be effective in influencing others to Christ? We seek quick, easy, and cheap fixes to many of the problems we face in ministry. We do not need another conference to make our ministry more effective; we just need more of the Spirit of God setting our hearts on fire. The answer is simple—but it is not cheap.

The final phase of Chadwick's life was spent as principal of Cliff College, a Methodist training school for preachers, and it was here that he wrote *The Way to Pentecost*. In it he said:

> I owe everything to the gift of Pentecost. For fifty days the facts of the Gospel were complete, but no conversions were recorded. Pentecost registered three thousand souls. It is by fire

that a holy passion is kindled in the soul whereby we live the life of God. The soul's safety is in its heat. Truth without enthusiasm, morality without emotion, ritual without soul, make for a Church without power . . . Destitute of the Fire of God, nothing else counts; possessing Fire, nothing else matters.⁷

Genuine movements of the Holy Spirit are special. They can be facilitated by our patterns and practices of worship, but they cannot be created or controlled by them. If the conditions are right, spontaneous combustion occurs. History seems to teach us that significant outpourings of the Holy Spirit follow after intense seeking after God. We can't program the baptism of the Holy Spirit, but we can earnestly seek it in our hunger for God and His holy fire.

Early in my ministry, I moved to a new pastorate and showed up Sunday morning for my first sermon. I had prepared what I believed to be God's word for the people that day. Before the service began I was informed by a fervent worshiper that they had not allowed the pastor to preach for the past three weeks and they expected there would be no preaching on this day. I guess my reputation had preceded me and they figured they could do without whatever it was I had planned to say. They had discovered the secret for stirring up the people, so I was informed that the time would be spent singing and testifying. I guess I had misunderstood what God wanted me to share because according to them there would be no sharing on this day. True to their word, they took over the service. True to my conscience, I managed to get my voice into the mix, and I delivered what I believed to be a word from God. Some thought I squelched the Spirit that day. Some thought the Spirit finally had an opportunity to get into the service.

> Genuine movements of the Holy Spirit are special. They can be facilitated by our patterns and practices of worship, but they cannot be created or controlled by them.

Worship leaders have the awesome responsibility of cooperating with the Holy Spirit in keeping the Ancient Fire active in individual lives and in corporate worship. You never want to be guilty of quenching the Spirit or hindering His work by your use of meaningless practice or by constructing boxes designed to control or contain Him. Sometimes, when the wind is blowing, it is hard to control fire and it can quickly get out of control. Come, Holy Spirit, and let your wind blow across our parched worship services and set them aflame as you baptize us with fire. Send the rain! Send the fire!

Reflection

- What are your church's beliefs and practices regarding baptism? Have you developed your own conviction regarding baptism?

- When was the last service of baptism in your church? How could it be made more meaningful for both the individual being baptized and the community participating in the event?

- Baptism follows conversion. What are you doing in your church to produce new converts?

Moving Forward

- Encourage new converts to be baptized, and tell them why this is so important.

- Schedule a baptism service, announce it publicly, and invite people to talk to you about their desire to be baptized.

- Schedule a class to inform candidates for baptism about the significance of baptism.

- Be clear in your heart and mind about your theological understanding of infant baptism so you can advise parents toward baptism or dedication for their children.

- Offer the opportunity for those who were baptized as infants to affirm that act by their parents, making their own covenant as a public declaration.

- Preach and teach the possibility of and necessity of baptism with the Holy Spirit.

ELEVEN

> "For this reason I remind you to fan into flame the gift of God, which is in you through the laying on of my hands. For God did not give us a spirit of timidity, but a spirit of power, of love and of self-discipline." —2 Tim. 1:6-7

Fan into Flame the Gift of God

The most impressive worship practices will never compensate for an absence of fire in the spirit of those who are responsible for leading worship. It is hard to keep the fire on the altar burning if you do not keep the flame burning in your own spirit.

In the natural world, fire gradually consumes the substance on which it feeds and eventually dies out, if new fuel is not added. Unless attention is given, the fire in the heart of a pastor will die out as well. Timothy was a protégé of Paul, and both New Testament letters to him are full of instructions from a seasoned veteran to an emerging pastor-leader. Paul underscored the need for Timothy to be assured of his calling, to develop competencies, to mature in character, and to love his community. As important as these requirements were for effective ministry, transcending them was Paul's exhortation to Timothy to "fan into flame the gift of God" (2 Tim. 1:6).

Every Sunday morning I encountered a venerable member on the way from my study to the passageway that led behind the platform where I led worship and proclaimed God's Word. This great church motivated me to want to give my best as I prepared for the awesome responsibility of connecting the people with God. But there was another motivation that came from knowing I would face this man every Sunday, and I would have to respond with integrity to the only words he would speak to me. It was the same question every week. He would look me in the eye and ask, "Pastor, is it burning?"

Admittedly, some weeks were so draining that it burned less than other weeks. But I understood the reason for this man's question, and it became a point of accountability for me. If the fire was not burning in my spirit, there wouldn't be much fire kindled in the worship service. John Wesley once admonished his preachers: "Catch on fire with enthusiasm and people will come for miles to watch you burn."[1]

Back in the 1970s, a religious fanatic made the news by setting himself on fire to protest something. I was talking about it at the local Rotary club while the woman who served our lunch was setting things up. She overheard the conversation and knowing I was a pastor, said, "If you would set yourself on fire next Sunday, I would come and watch you burn." I think she intended a spiritual application, but any way I might take it, there was a desire to see some fire in the pulpit.

> Catch on fire with enthusiasm and people will come for miles to watch you burn.
>
> —JOHN WESLEY

At the age of five, Wesley was rescued from the burning home in Epworth where his father was rector. His rescue from the fire impressed him deeply and caused him to believe that God had set him apart in a special way, as a "brand plucked from the burning." You could say that Wesley was a smoldering brand through a few years of preaching with varied degrees of effectiveness, until the flame was fanned and ignited in his heart in a way that would forever change his ministry. In his words,

> In the evening I went very unwillingly to a society in Aldersgate Street where one was reading Luther's preface to the Epistle to the Romans. About a quarter before nine, while he was describing the change which God works in the heart through faith in Christ, I felt my heart strangely warmed.[2]

The Fire of Passion

When the presence and power of God are experienced in the heart of a pastor, it ignites a secondary fire that is called *passion*. Passion is intense enthusiasm or interest. Related words include: fervor, obsession, excitement, enthusiasm, zeal, delight, and ardor. Paul issued the challenge: "Never be lacking in zeal, but keep your spiritual fervor, serving the Lord" (Rom. 12:11). This is different and greater than the enthusiasm you might demonstrate at a ballgame or feel about your favorite pastime. This is passion that is ignited by the Spirit of God—the Ancient Fire.

> When the presence and power of God are experienced in the heart of a pastor, it ignites a secondary fire that is called *passion*.

The fire the priests were to keep burning was a fire that had its origin in God. Do you remember the time in your life when the presence, glory, and blessing of God first came upon you? You will quickly learn in your ministry that you can't replicate the fire from God. No amount of personal charisma, spiritual gymnastics, or animated programming can compensate for a lack of fire from God. You may have felt the first spark of the flame of God in your spirit when you placed your faith in Christ for your salvation. Fuel was added to the fire when you sensed

God's call on your life to give yourself to the vocation of ministry. You felt God burning hot in your spirit the first time you stepped into the pulpit at your first pastoral assignment. Do you remember? Is the flame burning as hotly now as it was in those special times in the past? Do you need to stir up the fire again and fan it into flame?

I was talking with a friend about the leadership effectiveness of some pastors and the ineffectiveness of others. From his perspective, he said he saw fairly equal aptitudes among most pastors that he knew. But he saw other attitudinal and motivational qualities that varied significantly and affected their effectiveness. His comment on the matter was: "If your wood is wet, it is going to be hard to keep a fire burning."

A major concern of pastors should be to keep the wood from getting wet. Effectiveness in ministry is certainly related to the possession of certain ministerial skills—competencies. But no academic degree or skill acquisition can compensate for an absence of the "gift of God." H.B. London says, "The energizing Spirit of Christ makes high-achievement ministry possible—even in the toughest of times and in the hardest of places."[3] And he says, "For pastors who do their work continually in a world of half-hearted commitments, moral bankruptcies, devastating sins and dysfunctional people, spiritual dryness and emotional starvation are occupational land mines."[4] Spiritual dryness equates to having your wood wet.

Within the church, we too often want to make effective pastoral leadership to be:

- a set of skills to be acquired,
- a personality to be imitated,
- a set of strategies to be implemented, or
- seven habits to be cultivated.

Leadership may involve those things, but if there is no fire on the altar of the leader's heart, there is no effective spiritual leadership in the church.

You cannot over emphasize the necessity of vital spirituality and passion in those who lead others in worship. If the fire on the altar is to be kept burning continuously, there must be uninterrupted fire in the heart of the worship leader. As London said, "For too long pastors have short-changed themselves by separating personal holiness from the practice of ministry, competency from character and service from spirituality."[5]

In Exodus 28, God gave great detail concerning the attire and the procedures for Aaron and his sons as they cared for the fire and ashes on the altar and gave leadership to worship. Their consecration and purification was of highest importance. Their personal preparation was to be attended to before they were allowed to attend to their priestly responsibilities. Offering sacrifice and entering the presence of God carelessly and with personal un-atoned sin was punishable by death. Now that would be fairly effective extrinsic motivation!

Flickering Flames

Some people have enough natural talent and personal charisma to create what may appear on the surface to be effective ministries. But in time, the absence of spiritual fire will manifest itself and too much is at stake for any minister to attempt to make things happen by their own giftedness. The fire of God in the heart of a leader is critical because:

- Leaders must do things that require more than they have to offer.
- Leaders must discern what should remain unchanged in a world of continuous and deep change.
- Leaders must distinguish between things that are core and things that are peripheral—and keep core things core.

- Leaders must be motivated by vision through the windshield rather than reflection through the rearview mirror.
- Leaders must not be satisfied with things as they are but must see things as they could be.
- Leaders must be convinced that if things could be better, they should be better.
- Leaders must be passionate about ensuring that what should be better will become better.
- Leaders must be renewed constantly while working in situations and with people that are draining and depleting.

The fire of God once experienced needs to be given constant attention. Busy pastors must not neglect fanning the flame. Keeping the fire burning in a leader's heart can be difficult because of:

- Distraction—while busy with other things, the fire can burn itself out.
- Self-sufficiency—we think we can do without the fire.
- Multitude of responsibilities—ministry can become so crowded that there is no room for the fire to breathe.
- Discouragement—the great plague affecting many pastors is discouragement that throws water on their fire.
- Routine—we can grow tired doing the things necessary to keep the fire going. Continuous is a long time and requires a lot of attention. Spiritual disciplines require discipline, and that is hard to maintain over time.
- Spiritual attack—if the Enemy can diminish a leader's effectiveness or cause a loss of passion, a lot of damage can be done. Working the front lines of battle can be spiritually draining.

God wants to work with people who make partnership with Him their passionate focus. Too often in the church, we want quick fixes to our personal and corporate problems and lack of effectiveness. We find it easier to reorganize structures, replace people and programs, or rewrite procedures and practices while God wants to renew and rekindle the fire in us so our structures, programs, and practices have a spark of the Divine in them.

Maintaining Spiritual Vitality

Some materials, such as asbestos, are non-combustible. Missionary Jim Elliot, who gave up his life while attempting to minister to the Auca Indians, said, "He [God] makes His ministers a flame of fire. Am I ignitable? God deliver me from the dread asbestos of 'other things.' Saturate me with the oil of the Spirit that I may be aflame . . . Make me thy fuel, Flame of God."[6]

A pile of "other things" can become asbestos in the soul. It happens to pastors when their plate is full but their cup is empty. Ministry is most effective when it comes from the overflow of a person's life—when one's cup is overflowing. However, many pastors experience more overwork than overflow. Gary McIntosh says, "In this demanding environment, the press of church affairs often squeezes communion with God out of a pastor's schedule."[7] We can neglect in our lives the very things we know and teach that others need to retain spiritual vitality. The fire that once burned hot can die down to a flickering flame and smoldering smoke.

Ordination

Ordination to Christian ministry was a fiery moment in my spiritual journey. It was more than a final step in a credentialing process or a stamp of endorsement by my church. For me, it was a moment of enduement—a gift of grace that contributed to the fire and passion of ministry in me. When the Bible was placed in my hand with the command to "Take authority and preach the Word," I sensed the weight of that responsibility. When the hands of the elders were placed on me with the prayer that I be "clothed with righteousness and the power of the Holy Spirit," I sensed a passion for ministry build within me. It was more than meaningless ritual. It was a moment of fanning the flame of the Ancient Fire in me.

Our pragmatic and utilitarian age, combined with the intentional effort to elevate the ministry of laity in the church, have reduced the significance of ordination. For a number of years, I served in the denominational office that had the responsibility of overseeing the processes of ministerial preparation and credentialing. I regularly needed to defend the church's insistence on a prepared ministry. There were ministerial candidates who felt they did not need the endorsement of the church and ordination meant little more to them than a piece of paper on the wall and unnecessary hoops to jump through, both educationally and experientially. My heart ached for them. I knew they were going to be more dependent upon the competencies, experiences, and relational maturity that could be fuel for the fire of God than they presently realized. Preparation of the hand and heart requires a certain amount of time that when rushed can result in ineffectiveness and ultimate tragedy. There are no shortcuts to ordination, and no shortcuts in experiencing the flame of God in the human heart.

> No amount of personal charisma, spiritual gymnastics, or animated programming can compensate for a lack of fire from God.

The laying on of hands in the New Testament church was both a signal of separation to sacred service and a means through which the power of the Spirit came to rest upon the candidate. Timothy experienced it when the elders of the church laid hands on him—a fire was ignited in him and he was gifted for Spirit-empowered ministry. No dead, meaningless ritual here. Ordination continues as a ritual of the church through which the Ancient Fire ignites passion in the spirit of His servants so they can minister in the name of Christ with effectiveness. It is more than the completion of required courses, some in-service practice, and a successful interview with a board that grants approval. It is God working through the agencies of His church to set apart persons for ministry and equip them with passion and power.

Personal Preparation

Paul encouraged Timothy in his responsibility to fan the flame that God had ignited in him, and then he said, "Train yourself to be godly" (1 Tim. 4:7). This was a mandate, not a subtle suggestion. Fanning the flame and keeping the flame burning requires taking personal responsibility for establishing the patterns that develop and maintain vital spirituality. Before leading others in spiritual life-sustaining ritual, pastors must find the rhythm of dynamic ritual in their own lives. Charles Haddon Spurgeon once said that the person "who guides others into the presence of the King must have journeyed far into the King's country and often looked upon his face."[8] Mature Christians result from being ministered to by spiritually mature pastors and churches that are on fire for God are led by pastors who are on fire.

> If the fire on the altar is to be kept burning continuously, there must be uninterrupted fire in the heart of the worship leader.

Means of Grace

The spiritual disciplines that we encourage others to develop must characterize our spiritual walk as well. The disciples were just beginning their ministry after Jesus' departure, and the church was in its infancy, when the first test came to spiritual leadership. It came as the church began to demonstrate its love for the needy by providing food for the widows. The disciples realized the demands being placed on them were taking them away from the critical need of personal engagement with God. The solution was to appoint deacons who could care for the compassionate ministries of the church so the Twelve could give their "attention to prayer and the ministry of the word" (see Acts 6:2–4). Spiritually starving people cannot be fed by pastors who themselves have not fed on the Word of God. They cannot be led to connect with God by pastors who have not been in connection with God.

I transitioned from the pastorate, where I prepared for three or more speaking opportunities each week, to a denominational leadership position where speaking became less frequent. I came to realize that my Bible reading had become a ritual for developing sermons, not for developing my spiritual life. As I read, I was always looking for the next sermon and homiletically analyzing the text rather than breathing it in devotionally and feeding my spirit with it. I was reading with an eye on what the people needed rather than what I needed, and if I didn't need to come up with a sermon, then reading the Bible was not the pressing necessity that it had been. I came to realize that I could be in God's Word on a regular basis without allowing it to fan the flame in my own spirit. I had to take responsibility to feed myself first before I could feed others. It was like I had often been told on airplanes, "If the oxygen mask drops down in front of you, put yours on first before you help others." If you do not take in needed oxygen, you will be unable to help others take in oxygen.

Feeding on the Word of God is only one of several means of grace in which pastors need to be engaged. Regarding means of grace, Wesley wrote:

> By "means of grace" I understand outward signs, words, or actions, ordained of God, and appointed for this end, to be the ordinary channels whereby he might convey to men, preventing, justifying, or sanctifying grace. I use this expression, means of grace, because I know none better; and because it has been generally used in the Christian church for many ages;—in particular by our own Church, which directs us to bless God both for the means of grace, and hope of glory; and teaches us, that a sacrament is an outward sign of inward grace, and a means whereby we receive the same. The chief of these means are prayer, whether in secret or with the great congregation; searching the Scriptures (which implies reading, hearing, and meditating thereon); and receiving the Lord's Supper, eating bread and drinking wine in remembrance of Him: And these we believe to be ordained of God, as the ordinary channels of conveying his grace to the souls of men.[9]

It is much easier to tell others what they need to do than for us to do it ourselves. And if we believe that for some reason we do not need to do those things, we are wrong—dead wrong.

Intimacy with God

Pastors can slip into being religious hucksters, hawking their spiritual wares and promoting the next big program, event, or great sermon series. They can promote without participating in the very things they are trying to get others to do. Intimacy with God is not easily maintained in most ministers' schedules. John Mott said:

> The men that will change the colleges and seminaries here represented are the men that will spend the most time alone with God. It takes time for the fires to burn. It takes time for God to draw near and for us to know that He is there. It takes time to assimilate His truth. You ask me, How much time? I do not know. I know it means time enough to forget time.[10]

Philip Yancey has said, "God doesn't care so much about being analyzed. Mainly, he wants to be loved."[11] When we become more analyzers than lovers of God, it is time to fan into flame the gift of God.

Oswald Chambers said, "It is a joy to Jesus when a person takes time to walk more intimately with Him. The bearing of fruit is always shown in Scripture to be a visible result of an intimate relationship with Jesus Christ."[12]

E.M. Bounds said,

> Love is kindled in a flame, and ardency is its life. Flame is the air which true Christian experience breathes. It feeds on fire; it can withstand anything rather than a feeble flame; but when the surrounding atmosphere is frigid or lukewarm, it dies, chilled and starved to its vitals. True prayer must be aflame.[13]

Fanning the Flame

Fire in a leader's soul is the result of the present presence and blessing of God. What was started must be retained. Pastors must consistently:

- seek God's presence and blessing, making Him the most desired thing in their life and ministry;

- guard their spirit so no attitude or motive displeasing to Him gets a foothold in them;
- watch their actions so nothing blocks the free flow of His Spirit in their life;
- screen their relationships to be sure no one crowds Him out or no impropriety is hidden in a closet of their life;
- "Let the word of Christ dwell in [them] richly" (Col. 3:16); and
- keep declaring their dependence upon God—and mean it. You can try to move your people by leveraging your natural ability and trumped-up charisma. You can only lead your people spiritually when you have the mind and Spirit of Christ.

The Israelites were in captivity in Egypt. Moses was in the wilderness tending the flocks of his father-in-law when he encountered God who spoke to him from a flaming bush. Moses was told to go to Pharaoh and demand that he let the people of God go. At this point in time it was not so they could start the trek to the Promised Land. God wanted the people to go into the wilderness to worship. It was in the wilderness that Moses met with God, and now God wanted Moses to lead the people out into the wilderness to connect with Him in worship.

> The fire of God once experienced needs to be given constant attention. Busy pastors must not neglect fanning the flame.

The man who met with God was to lead others to meet with God. This is how it is to be. Those who lead others to connect with God should already have connected with Him. They know where God is because they have been there. They have spoken with Him. They have heard from Him. They have been in touch with the Ancient Fire and are prepared to lead others to feel His flame igniting their spirits.

The Sabbath

The flame flickers and burns low when pastors fail to maintain the ritual of a Sabbath day each week. Sundays are days for giving out, not taking in. Sure, it is energizing to meet with your people, invest in their lives, celebrate life with them, and worship with them. But every pastor knows the weariness that settles in all the way to the bone when Sunday evening comes. It is a tiredness that one night of sleep will not remove. As much as you love your work, you need a day for personal renewal. And the need for a Sabbath day grows deeper if you have developed a jaundiced view of your work because of the energy sappers that we will always have with us.

Governing boards may need to insist that their pastors establish a personal Sabbath each week—and hold them accountable to take it. There is far more support for this among parishioners than pastors may expect. There is a new awareness for creation care among emerging generations and they are reaching back to the Sabbath rituals of the Old Testament, realizing that God built into all of nature—including persons, their flocks, and their fields—a need for periodic rest and renewal. Fruitfulness is not the result of pushing beyond sensible limits. Build the rhythm and ritual of the Sabbath in your life and both you and your people will be better because of it.

God has called you into His service. He has gifted you in unique ways to fulfill His purposes in you and through your ministry. He has used the church to equip you and to endorse you for ministry. He has ignited the flame of passion in your spirit through the indwelling ministry of His Holy Spirit. It is now your responsibility to keep the fire burning. Fan into flame the gift that is in you.

Reflection

- When were the great spiritual moments in your life when your passion for God was ignited?

- How do you specifically and intentionally keep the fire burning in your own soul?

- Where in your ministry do you find passion motivating and energizing you?

- On a scale of one to ten, with ten being the highest, where would you rate your level of intimacy with God? What could you do to improve your rating?

- Have you been protecting your mind from impure thoughts, your heart from alienating affections, and your spirit from attitudes that compete against the Spirit of Christ?

Moving Forward

- Establish spiritual disciplines and schedule the times you will practice them. Some of these times will be daily, some weekly, and some less frequently, but perhaps with greater intensity and extended in duration.

- Locate a place where you can get alone with God. Try to cultivate the discipline of silence and solitude as a means of increasing your focus on God and what He wants to say to you.

- Develop a close mentor or confidant—one to whom you can go when you sense the flame beginning to flicker. Be transparent about your spiritual life and allow this person to speak into your life and partner with you in prayer.

TWELVE

"Every day they continued to meet together in the temple courts. They broke bread in their homes and ate together with glad and sincere hearts, praising God and enjoying the favor of all the people. And the Lord added to their number daily those who were being saved." —Acts 2:46-47

The Lord Added to Their Number

People who hang around a fire are warmed by it, and if they get close enough, they will catch on fire too, because fire ignites more fire. Fire has an insatiable hunger to reproduce itself. If the Ancient Fire accompanies our worship practices, it will result in more people set on fire for God. Dynamic worship will have evangelism as one of its outcomes.

Most pastors like crowds. Get a bunch of pastors together and one of the first questions asked will be, "How many did you have in church last Sunday?" If the number was good, you will get a quantitative number—"We are breaking all kind of records. We are fifty ahead of this time a year ago." If the number was not so good, you will get a qualitative reply—"The crowd was down, but there sure was a good spirit in the service." It is wonderful when there is a convergence of spirit and numbers. That's what happened following the Pentecost birthday of the church. It can happen today too. People are attracted to fire.

Pastors often like to talk about evangelism more than they like to do evangelism. It is great when crowds gather and people get saved without having to do a lot to get it to happen—like going out where the people are and doing evangelism. We would rather have the kind of worship service that can draw people in—services that will attract the un-churched and with which they will feel comfortable.

What attracts people to a Christian community? We have used our places, programs, people, and preachers to draw others to us. We have given attention to our sacred places, in terms of scouting out visible and accessible locations and constructing impressive architecture. We have developed programs designed to meet felt needs or attract interest. We have leveraged the influence of people to draw others—encouraging the faithful to bring others, or featuring recognizable personalities. Some churches are fortunate to have unusually gifted preachers whose reputation for delivering great sermons has been a draw. There are people out there who need what we have to offer. In some respects, they are consumers and we try to maximize the ways in which we can get them to come to us and discover our product.

> Fire has an insatiable hunger to reproduce itself. If the Ancient Fire accompanies our worship practices, it will result in more people set on fire for God.

Almost twenty years ago, Elmer Towns summarized what the church-going consumer was looking for, and I think his observations generally still hold true:

> America's Protestants choose churches on the basis of what affirms us, entertains us, satisfies us or makes us feel good about God and ourselves. If we recognize church worshipers as

consumers, we will recognize church programs as menus, and types of worship as the main entrees in the restaurant . . . consumers go where the menus fit their taste . . . the church menus Americans seek are not filled with doctrinal options but with a variety of worship options. Americans go where they feel comfortable with the style of worship that best reflects their inclinations and temperament.[1]

Attraction Evangelism

The church has both inward and outward focus. The soul of the inward focus of the church is worship. Without vital and vibrant connection with God, the outward focus is lost. Worship gives energy and meaning to evangelism and to compassionate ministry.

> Worship gives energy and meaning to evangelism and to compassionate ministry.

Attraction evangelism is valid, but dangerous if not carried out with the right motivation. If we are not careful, we can be more concerned as to whether outsiders can identify with the beat of the music than if they can hear the voice of God.

My most recent pastorate was in a rapidly growing suburban area. We planted the church at the outer edges of the urban sprawl, prior to the arrival of the new homesteaders. It was no small miracle that God provided us with ten acres of corn field that would soon become prime real estate. We built a modest first phase and almost immediately people began stopping in. They didn't come because they knew anything about us—we just had located in a visible place, they were looking for a church home, and they stopped to give us a try. Their coming wasn't even a strategic evangelistic outreach plan on our part. The location drew them in. There is something to be said for location, location, location. But location is not the final word to be said about reaching and evangelizing people.

Places may attract because of convenience, but places do not keep people—or necessarily show them God. God is all about establishing relationship, and He uses human relationships to facilitate the development of a relationship with Him. The big shift between the Old Testament temple worship and the New Testament church worship was that community and communion became more important than place. Jesus emphasized this when He told the woman at the well, "A time is coming when you will worship the Father neither on this mountain nor in Jerusalem . . . true worshipers will worship the Father in spirit and truth." (John 4:21, 23). Moved by the Spirit, believers have moved in to sanctify and to occupy spaces previously occupied by secular enterprises. Warehouses, shopping centers, schools, barns, abandoned cathedrals, shade trees, tin roofs with no sides—all have become sacred spaces. What takes place is more important than where it takes place.

Our practical, multi-purpose worship centers have resulted in far too few sacred places in our world—places that have no other purpose but to be our place to meet God. I have a deep appreciation for architecture, art and worship elements that speak of God and direct my attention toward him. However, I know that ultimately worship is about relationship, not about what I surround myself with as I seek God. A candle may help set a mood, but its flame is not what will warm my spirit.

Most pastors are motivated to grow their churches numerically, and they can employ a wide range of strategies to accomplish this. The motivation, however, is not to fill up space, but to fill empty souls with God. As C. Kirk Hadaway said, "We should be less concerned about making churches full of people and more concerned about making people full of God."[2]

Incendiary Fellowship

Elton Trueblood referred to the Spirit-enabled church as "the incendiary fellowship."³ When the Holy Spirit fills individuals and they join their lives and spirits in worship, they become an on-fire church. When the church is on fire, people are attracted to its fellowship, as a moth is to a flame. Revivalist Leonard Ravenhill said, "You never have to advertise a fire. You don't have to advertise it in the news paper, forget it. You let the glory of the Lord fill the temple; people will come from hundreds of miles."⁴

> The Spirit of God wants to work His way through the uniqueness of who we are to make the grace and power of God visible and attractive to those who do not know Him.

When the Holy Spirit came upon the waiting believers at Pentecost, they were set ablaze, and those who had come to Jerusalem to observe Pentecost were attracted to them to see what was happening. These disciples certainly went into all the world as Jesus had commissioned them, but there was something about them that attracted people to go to them. The Spirit came in before the believers went out, and when the Spirit came in, the resulting fire attracted others. Attraction evangelism preceded itinerate evangelism. There is an attractiveness to authentic, dynamic worship. Samuel Chadwick said:

> Spirit filled souls are ablaze for God. They love with a love that glows. They serve with a faith that kindles. They serve with a devotion that consumes. They hate sin with fierceness that burns. They rejoice with a joy that radiates. Love is perfected in the fire of God.⁵

When love is genuine and unconditional, it draws people in.

That They May See

Jesus said about His followers:

> You are the light of the world. A city on a hill cannot be hidden. Neither do people light a lamp and put it under a bowl. Instead they put it on its stand, and it gives light to everyone in the house. In the same way, let your light shine before men, that they may see your good deeds and praise your Father in heaven. (Matt. 5:14–16)

The fire of God's Spirit is the light within us that is to shine out for others to see. We are not simply to gain people's respect because we are good, upright people. That may influence, but not illuminate. Others are to see our good deeds and praise our Father, not us. Our transformed, illuminated lives are to guide people to see our Father and come to know Him. The Spirit of God wants to work His way through the uniqueness of who we are to make the grace and power of God visible and attractive to those who do not know Him. Dwight L. Moody said, "We are told to let our light shine, and if it does, we won't need to tell anybody it does. Lighthouses don't fire cannons to call attention to their shining—they just shine."[6]

We have been in candle lighting services, usually on Christmas Eve, when a flame is taken from the Christ candle in the center of the Advent wreath and used to pass the flame among the worshipers waiting in darkness, until every candle is lit. Then we have been asked to raise our candles and suddenly the whole room comes alive with light from every candle. It is a visible symbol of the effect of displaying the flame God has ignited in each of us—a flame that has the capacity to attract and to lead people to the Light of the World and to the Ancient Flame.

The effectiveness of our collective flames is only possible when individuals decide: "This little light of mine, I'm going to let it shine." Our candle must not be covered up in some dark corner of our inner life, but it must be allowed to shine out so others might see. Individuals must let their light shine so the church might become the "city on a hill that cannot be hidden." When your light is combined with my light, we can significantly push back more darkness.

Worship Evangelism

God's agenda for the church always includes witness to the world, whether the church is involved in worship, fellowship, nurture, outreach, or service. His charge to His disciples prior to His ascension was to "go and make disciples of all nations, baptizing them in the name of the Father and of the Son and of the Holy Spirit, and teaching them to obey everything I have commanded you" (Matt. 28:19–20).

The Sunday school movement began in England in the mid-eighteenth century as a means of evangelism through education, primarily with children. For nearly two centuries, Sunday school was the entry point to the more full-orbed ministries of the church. Contests and gimmicks, featuring all kinds of bizarre behavior, were conducted as a means of drawing a crowd for the greater purpose of presenting the gospel. I am embarrassed now by some of the antics that accompanied the promotional stunts designed to attract people. The motive was good, but now it seems the tactics were rather misguided.

A shift began during the last quarter of the twentieth century. In most places, Sunday school lost its popularity and no longer brought in the crowds. Christian education, which included weeknight activities, small groups, and a broad spectrum of programs took on greater prominence but never seemed to have the power of attraction that Sunday school had. And then, fueled by the effectiveness of mega-churches in drawing big crowds through seeker sensitive programming, the church shifted to the worship service as the point of entry. If people could be drawn to the church to have an experience that was relevant to them with their secular orientation, they could be led into a process of coming to know Christ.

The shift to use Sunday morning worship as the primary means of attraction evangelism has created a lot of the tension presently being experienced in many churches. If the worship service is designed for the non-believer, when does the believer worship? If worship is an activity of a child of God of which a non-believer is incapable, should the worship hour be taken over for the sake of those unable to worship?

Our worship services should give God's people opportunity to truly and fully worship, and that worship should in turn become the light that is not hidden, but which causes the world to see God through the lives of the worshipers. Worship evangelism should be the result of spontaneous combustion. All of the elements are present for fire to break out to ignite a flame in the heart of spiritually hungry, seeking persons. Believers are acknowledging God with their worship and praise. The light of their lives, the love of their fellowship, and the influence of the church draws non-believers and illuminates the way toward God. The testimony of transformation ignites hope in those who are without God in their world.

> God's agenda for the church always includes witness to the world, whether the church is involved in worship, fellowship, nurture, outreach, or service.

The Holy Spirit that is moving through God's people creates an environment much like a wild fire, where the wind blows a spark, or the heat increases to the point that the flame jumps from what is burning to that which isn't and causes combustion to occur. If believers are not provided the opportunity to worship, God cannot use their combined flames to attract non-believers to the source of their fire. Worship is for believers, and through the lifting up of Christ in their worship, others can be drawn to Him.

Altar Call

The only furnishing in the tabernacle Holy of Holies, and later in the temple, was the ark of the covenant. It was a wooden box covered with gold in which was a bowl of manna, the tablets of law, and Aaron's staff. Its gold-covered lid had two carved angels on it facing each other with their wings overshadowing the lid. God called the place between the wings "the mercy seat." It was there that God said He would meet with His people (Ex. 25). Atonement was completed on the altar and made possible a place at the ark for a mercy meeting between God and sinner. The atonement provided a place at which a person could meet with God and experience His forgiveness.

> Our worship services should give God's people opportunity to truly and fully worship, and that worship should in turn become the light that is not hidden, but which causes the world to see God through the lives of the worshipers.

Coming to God as a repentant sinner seeking salvation is a matter of the heart, but physical action seems to facilitate and accommodate this action of the heart. American revivalism realized physical-spiritual connection and created the mourner's bench as a place where people could go and meet with God. It was little more than a low railing where guilt-ridden sinners could kneel to confess their sins and find God. Evangelistic services ended with a call to come forward to receive Christ. The mourner's bench evolved into a more tasteful altar, and the altar call became a standard ritual in the life of the evangelical church.

Preaching for a verdict has been a standard for churches that grew out of the revivalist and holiness movements of the 1800s. The ritual of the altar call has undergone a number of modifications in an effort to be less offensive and more seeker sensitive. Now seekers are asked to raise their hands, to make eye contact with the preacher, to indicate their need on a card, to come to a side room after the service, to silently join the preacher in reciting the sinner's prayer, or to look up one of the pastoral staff for instruction in how to become a Christian after the service.

Calling for people to make a commitment to follow Christ remains a part of worship evangelism. One church that is a rapidly growing, multi-venue congregation is 12Stone Community Church in Lawrenceville, Georgia. It is contemporary and is attracting many non-churched people through its dynamic worship experiences. The pastor, Kevin Myers, is not content to attract people to the church but has a passion to connect people to Christ. He provides a variety of means by which persons who want to meet with God can be invited to do so. In one service, he had a bridge constructed and placed on the stage. He challenged those who wanted to find new life in Christ to come to the stage, cross over the bridge, and meet Him on the other side. Seekers identified with the gap that existed between them and God. Crossing over the bridge become a symbol to them of making a decision and taking the steps to meet with God, closing the gap through the sacrifice of Christ, experiencing forgiveness, and moving into a new changed life on the other side. Scores of people responded to a new expression of an old ritual of "coming forward."

Probably the greatest regret I have of my years of ministry are the opportunities to call people to salvation in Christ that were lost. Leading people to Christ was a passion of my ministry and was practiced through Bible studies, personal encounters, and counseling opportunities. But in reflection, I think I viewed the times when there was no visible response to an invitation as being a personal failure, which then caused me to neglect future times of preaching for a verdict and calling for a public commitment. Consequently, I look at many of my sermons and ask "so what?" They were homiletically sound, alliteratively pleasing but the salvation objective was uncertain, and I am sure the result was less effective than God would have wanted for adding people to His church. I cannot go back and change the past, but I have asked God to forgive me for failing to give the opportunity for the Holy Spirit to move people toward a public confession of Christ and of their sinfulness.

Evangelism is the inevitable result of Spirit-filled worship. When people experience the Ancient Fire in worship, numbers will be added to the church as people come to Christ.

Reflection

- Would you characterize your church as growing, maintaining, or declining? What reasons do you give for the current status of your church?

- What attracts people to your church? Where is the entry point for most new persons who come to your church?

- In what ways do you give opportunity for people to respond to the salvation call from God?

Moving Forward

- Create a group of persons who can assist you in developing an intentional evangelism strategy for your church.

- Develop a strategy for moving people from attraction to assimilation into the church as fully functioning disciples of Christ.

- Learn to preach in a manner that requires a response, then provide a means for people to respond that is appropriate for the message and the setting.

THIRTEEN

"When Solomon finished praying, fire came down from heaven and consumed the burnt offering and the sacrifices, and the glory of the Lord filled the temple." —2 Chron. 7:1

The Glory of the Lord Filled the Temple

Everything else fades into insignificance when the glory of God is present, and there is within the spirit of God's people deep desire to see His glory fill the place where they worship. Lifeless routine and half-hearted performances do not capture the spirit of those who long to know God and experience His glory.

It could be that 2 Chronicles 7 contains a sequence that can be a recipe for dynamic worship. Sacrifices were offered. Prayer was made. Fire consumed. Glory filled the temple. And people worshiped:

> When all the Israelites saw the fire coming down and the glory of the LORD above the temple, they knelt on the pavement with their faces to the ground, and they worshiped and gave thanks to the LORD, saying, "He is good; his love endures forever." (2 Chron. 7:3)

We want to experience glory—things that stir us and amaze us. We can do our best to create stimulating experiences, but there are no substitutes for His glory, and there are no shortcuts to His glory. Before we can experience His glory, we must submit to His fire that consumes—consuming fire precedes glory. We must be willing for God to take the best we have to bring, consume it, and replace it with the best that He can bring. It is then that true worship captures a congregation. This is a sequence that leads us into worship.

We bring our best as a sacrifice.

We seek the Lord with all our heart.

We allow God to consume us and our offering.

He fills us and our place of meeting with His glory.

We worship as we recognize His presence, realize His power, and rejoice in His glory.

Do It Again

It is exciting when the Ancient Fire invades a worshiping congregation and the place is filled with His presence and power. I have been there and it is refreshing. I go from these encounters wishing I could replicate it over and over in places where there seems to be so little fire. However, experiences can't be stuffed into carry-out packages, and I don't have the power to replicate the experience, but God does. As much as we might want to be positive about our weekly worship experiences, the reality is that the fire from heaven does not come down every time we meet for worship. Why is that? What is different in the times and places when it does happen?

> Before we can experience His glory, we must submit to His fire that consumes—consuming fire precedes glory.

William Booth, founder of the Salvation Army, was interested in social reform and longed to do something to alleviate the suffering of the poor in England. He attended Wesley Chapel of Nottingham and was saved as a teenager. After that, he was often found kneeling at the front of the chapel, earnestly seeking after the Lord. A spirit-filled American evangelist visited Nottingham and preached the Wesleyan message of sanctification with great unction and power. This preaching made a great impression on young Booth and kindled a fire within him to win souls for Christ. God used Booth to help the poor and lead many people to Christ, and the movement he began in England remains as a worldwide ministry today. Many who have visited the chapel have been seen kneeling near a plaque that marks the spot where Booth sought the Lord. It is reported that one such person was heard praying. "O God, do it again! Do it again!"

> The God of fire is not limited to meeting His people and sharing His glory only in the past. What He has done, He can and will do again.

The God of fire is not limited to meeting His people and sharing His glory only in the past. What He has done, He can and will do again. And we cry, "O God, do it again!" This hunger to experience a fresh movement of the Holy Spirit is being voiced by contemporary worshipers. The song "Let Your Fire Fall" is not a song of days long passed, but a song made popular by contemporary musicians. It vocalizes the collective hunger of our age:

>   Come and show Your power as in days of old
>   Lord, Lord let Your fire fall
>   Burn up the idols of wood and stone
>   Lord, Lord let Your fire fall
>   We come before You Father

> We offer You our lives
> Our hearts are on Your altar
> Consume the sacrifice
> Lord, Lord let Your fire fall
> Lord, Lord let Your fire fall
>
> Come and show Your power in our midst today
> Lord, Lord let Your fire fall
> Holy Spirit come and have Your way
> Lord, Lord let Your fire fall
> Purify Your people
> Set our hearts aflame
> Give us holy passion
> Come and glorify Your name
> O Lord, Lord let Your fire fall
> Lord, Lord let Your fire fall[1]

God's people have a longing in their spirit to experience God in fresh and powerful ways—to see the glory and salvation of God. They have the kind of hunger for God that was demonstrated by Simeon who longed for the consolation of Israel, and this longing took him regularly to the temple. It was there Simeon encountered the infant Jesus who had been brought by His parents for presentation to the priests. "Simeon took him in his arms and praised God, saying: 'Sovereign Lord, as you have promised, you now dismiss your servant in peace. For my eyes have seen your salvation'" (Luke 2:28–30). It is not enough that the glory of God has been experienced by others in other times and in other places. Our eyes want to see His glory. Our spirits long to be ignited by His holy flame. Do it again, Lord! Do it again.

Thirteen

Prayer Precedes Fire

It was when Solomon finished praying that the fire came down. It was after being constantly in prayer that the fire fell on Pentecost. It was after prayer and fasting that the Holy Spirit came upon Barnabas and Saul and set them apart for service. It was after they prayed that the place was shaken where the disciples were huddled, the Holy Spirit filled them, and they broke huddle to speak boldly. God shows up where people earnestly seek Him.

The times of prayer during worship are not needless ritual, dutifully repeated. They are a part of the practice of seeking after God and asking Him to intervene in the usual and turn it into the unusual. We bring the wood and then ask Him to set it on fire.

In the early days of the church plant of which I was a part, we periodically conducted twenty-four-hour prayer vigils. We recognized that prayer was critical to our survival in those days. (We lose more than we realize when our churches get strong enough that we no longer sense the critical nature of prayer. Satisfaction with the status quo is a spiritual anesthetic that keeps us from feeling the pain of trying to go it alone without the supernatural—the pain that accompanies terminal illness and precedes death.) We had people sign up for one-hour segments to pray and write their thoughts in a prayer journal. The first few times, this prayer vigil took place wherever the participants wanted because we did not own a facility. Then we had them drive to the area where we were meeting in a school to pray for our church and the community in which we planned to locate. Later, they sat in their cars that were parked across the road from the corn field we wanted to purchase and where we would build a permanent church home. Later still, we cleared the corn from a space in the field where people could park their car and pray. A year later we were able to move through the cold, dark shell of a building and pray for the ministry that would someday be facilitated by our people through this facility. Then the day came when our prayer team sat in a nice room of the newly constructed building and focused their prayer on needy people and the effectiveness of outreach ministries. It was a journey of faith and of fervent prayer. The journey was full of challenges for which we did not have the capacity to overcome.

Those were days of divine intervention in the potential disasters that so often threaten church plants. God's miraculous provision always followed our time of fervent prayer. The bond between people in this newly established spiritual family became stronger and stronger as we joined in prayer and witnessed the hand of God at work. The spiral bound notebooks that were our prayer journals contain the powerful prayers and spiritual insights of people caught up in the passion of wanting to see the glory of the Lord filling His temple. Prayer is not a dead ritual. When people pray, God responds.

Sacrifice Precedes Glory

If we want to experience the fire of God and to see His glory, we must bring our best and be willing for Him to consume it on His altar. God is a consuming fire. No one or no thing is worthy of standing before His Holiness. Our best is required, but our best is not good enough. God will consume what we place on His altar, and we have to be willing to offer Him our best and let Him make it His and burn it up. We cannot glory in what we do in worship or we will never see His glory. We have to allow Him to consume our best performance. Our performances will never satisfy us as much as His performance will. Our most glorious productions, delivered with as much excellence as we are capable, have no

> If we want to experience the fire of God and to see His glory, we must bring our best and be willing for Him to consume it on His altar. God is a consuming fire.

glory unless His fire falls and consumes them, leaving everyone amazed at Him, not at us. It was the glory of God not the spotless sacrifice on the altar that caused the people of Israel to fall on their faces before the Lord, to worship, and to proclaim His goodness and love. Our acts of worship are our offering to God, and they are to be our best. But when placed on the altar, they become His, and if He is to get the glory, honor, and praise due Him, He will consume our offerings so we do not glory in them. It is an affront to God for us to praise the excellence of the offering someone gave, without seeing the God to whom it was to be given.

Hunger Precedes Holiness

Both the sacrifice and the one presenting that sacrifice are to be holy. Sanctification is the process that results in the condition of holiness. Sanctification is the work of God, taking what we offer to Him, making it His, setting it apart for His use, cleansing it of anything contrary to His nature and purpose, and blessing it with His Spirit. Sanctification produces holiness. Holiness and worship are inseparably joined. If you hunger to see the glory of God, you must first hunger for His holiness. Holiness is characterized by a hunger to know God in all of His transforming power that produces a relationship of mutual love that enriches, enables, and empowers. Holiness is the commitment to fulfill the commandment to love God with all of the heart, mind, soul, and strength. Holiness is a work of the Holy Spirit cleansing, filling, and empowering the human spirit to work, witness, and worship effectively. If you want to experience the glory of God in worship, first experience the glory of God in your own

> If you hunger to see the glory of God, you must first hunger for His holiness.

spirit. Hunger precedes holiness, and holiness gives legitimacy to worship. What God did at Pentecost, He will do again—in you and in your congregation of worshipers.

Passion for God

Too often we can be guilty of being too casual about worship. We allow it to become routine. We expect little when we enter, and we are not disappointed when we leave with what we expected. There is no passion, and we accept it. Excellence is absent, and we do not expect it to return any time soon. We are content to settle for mediocre offerings and no fire. We must make worshiping God our passion.

Prayer, sacrifice, hunger, passion—all precede the demonstration of God's presence and power. You want to know how to bring new life to your worship? Start doing your part and have faith that God will do His part. You will not experience His fire or see His glory simply by showing up and then wondering where God is.

The worship practices of cultures and generations may differ, but the Ancient Fire is the constant, connecting link between the ages. He is not confined to the language or rituals of any single group or time. The God who answers with fire is still energizing congregations today, and He can energize yours.

When the Service Begins

Worship and service are linked together. Those who worship God in spirit and in truth are to be lights in the world and salt in the earth. We gather to worship, and we scatter to serve. We come together to be enabled, and we leave to use our influence to transform our communities and culture. God's presence and power were never intended to be consumed. It is not good to be a spectator rather than a participant in worship, and it is worse to be a consumer not a distributor of the benefits of meeting with God. It is no cliché to say that the service does not begin at 10:30 on Sunday morning. The service begins when you leave the sanctuary where God has just touched your candle with the Ancient Fire.

The mantle has fallen on us to institute ritual that connects people to God. In order to do that, we need to:

- educate ourselves and our people about the need for and nature of real worship;
- discipline ourselves to give adequate time to plan and to prepare for our times of worship;
- be creative in communicating with contemporary people and connecting them with God;
- become students of our context—our people, our culture, the season, and current events.

There is power in how we lead worship if we team up with the Holy Spirit who can energize what we do so the Ancient Fire can be released to ignite our hearts in worship that pleases God, to renew our spirits, and to attract others to Him. Let us give ourselves to the joyful responsibility of keeping the fire burning continuously.

> Revive us again;
> Fill each heart with Thy love;
> May each soul be rekindled
> With fire from above.[2]

Reflection

- Do you approach your ministry and leadership of worship with optimism—with the belief that God is going to show up and do something wonderful?

- Where do you see God working in your church? How can you better communicate to your people these places where God is working so you can build enthusiasm and faith?

- Is there a desire for revival in your church? What can you do to stir up hunger for a new movement of God in your church?

Moving Forward

- Call your people to specific prayer and fasting for a fresh outpouring of God's Spirit that will light a fire in your worship and draw people to Christ.

- Schedule concentrated periods for prayer, such as a twenty-four-hour prayer vigil or a prayer walk around your church and through your community.

- Lead by example by being serious about worship, giving God your best, being willing to be consumed to glorify God, and by hungering and thirsting for God and His righteousness.

Notes

Introduction
1. Robert King, "Young Indianapolis Churchgoers Find Meaning Under the Archway," *Indianapolis Star*, Aug. 2, 2009, Section A.

Chapter 1
1. Wikipedia, "Fire (Classic Element)," http://en.wikipedia.org/wiki/Fire_(classical_element)#cite_note-F-0 (accessed February 11, 2009).
2. Charles B. Williams, *The New Testament, A Private Translation in the Language of the People* (Chicago: Moody Press, 1949), quoted in Charles W. Carter, *Hebrews: The Wesleyan Bible Commentary* (Grand Rapids, Mich.: Eerdmans, 1966), 170.
3. George Barna, *Revolution* (Wheaton, Ill.: Tyndale House, 2005), 31.

Chapter 2
1. Samuel Chadwick, *The Way to Pentecost* (Ft. Washington, Pa.: CLC, 2001), 49.

Chapter 3
1. Gary McIntosh and Robert Edmondson, *It Only Hurts on Monday* (Carol Stream, Ill.: ChurchSmart Resources, 1998), 14.
2. *The Discipline of The Wesleyan Church 2008* (Indianapolis, Ind.: Wesleyan Publishing House, 2008), 313:1.
3. Ibid., 725:5.
4. Ibid., 675.

Chapter 4
1. Robert E. Webber, *Ancient-Future Time: Forming Spirituality through the Christian Year* (Grand Rapids, Mich.: Baker, 2004), 11.

2. Constance Cherry, "Merging Tradition and Innovation in the Life of the Church" in *The Conviction of Things Not Seen*, Todd Johnson, ed. (Grand Rapids, Mich.: Brazos Press, 2002), 30.
3. Quoted by Lester Ruth in *The Conviction of Things Not Seen*, Todd Johnson, ed. (Grand Rapids, Mich.: Brazos Press, 2002), 41.
4. Ibid., 44.
5. Robert Rayburn, "The Purpose of Liturgy," www.faithtaccma.org (accessed May 23, 2009).
6. Christina Baldwin, http://www.quotes.net/quote/19522 (accessed May 23, 2009).

Chapter 5
1. Lutheran World Federation, "Nairobi Statement on Worship and Culture," http://www.worship.ca/docs/lwf_ns.html (accessed August 20, 2009).
2. Ibid.
3. Constance Cherry, "Merging Tradition and Innovation in the Life of the Church" in *The Conviction of Things Not Seen*, Todd Johnson, ed. (Grand Rapids, Mich.: Brazos Press, 2002), 32.
4. From John Wesley, *Select Hymns*, 1761, quoted in the preface of the United Methodist Hymnal (Nashville: United Methodist Publishing House, 1989), vii.

Chapter 6
1. "God, presence of," http://www.sermons.illustrations.com (accessed August 20, 2009).

Chapter 7
1. Charles W. Carter, *A Contemporary Wesleyan Theology* (Grand Rapids, Mich.: Francis Asbury Press, 1983), 267.
2. John Witvliet, "Beyond Style," in *The Conviction of Things Not Seen*, Todd Johnson, ed. (Grand Rapids, Mich.: Brazos Press, 2002), 71.
3. Samuel Chadwick, *The Way to Pentecost* (Berne, Ind : Light and Hope, 1937), 47.
4. H.B. London and Neil Wiseman, *Pastors at Greater Risk* (Ventura, Calif.: Regal, 2003), 302.
5. The Old Time Gospel, "Famous Quotes: Thoughts on Prayer, Revival & Missions," www.theoldtimegospel.org/dev/quote1b.htm (accessed August 18, 2009).

Chapter 8
1. Robert E. Webber, *Planning Blended Worship* (Nashville, Tenn.: Abingdon, 1998), 15.

2. Dennis Bratcher, *The Season of Advent: Anticipation and Hope* (Oklahoma City, Okla.: Christian Resource Institute, 2009). See also http://cresourcei.org/cyadvent.html (accessed July 20, 2009).
3. Ibid.
4. Franklin Segler, *Christian Worship* (Nashville: Broadman & Holman Publishers, 1996), 178.

Chapter 9

1. Joseph Pine II and James Gilmore, *The Experience Economy* (Boston: Harvard Business School Press, 1999), 3.
2. Keith Drury, *Holiness for Ordinary People, 25th Anniversary Edition* (Indianapolis, Ind.: Wesleyan Publishing House, 2009), 187.
3. John Wesley, "Sermon XVI, The Means of Grace," in *The Works of John Wesley, Third Edition* (Kansas City, Mo.: Beacon Hill, 1979), 187.
4. John Wesley, "Sermon CI, The Duty of Constant Communion," in *The Works of John Wesley, Third Edition* (Kansas City, Mo.: Beacon Hill, 1979), 148.

Chapter 10

1. Roy Staples, *Outward Sign of an Inward Grace* (Kansas City, Mo.: Beacon Hill, 1991), 21.
2. *The Discipline of The Wesleyan Church 2008* (Indianapolis, Ind.: Wesleyan Publishing House, 2008), 290.
3. Lyle Williams, unpublished study paper presented at a Consultation on Church Doctrines in 1974.
4. *Discipline*, 5550.
5. Samuel Chadwick, *The Way to Pentecost* (Berne, Ind.: Light and Hope, 1937), 50.
6. Ibid., 17.
7. Ibid.

Chapter 11

1. John Wesley, http://quotationsbook.com/quote/12614/ (accessed August 18, 2009).
2. The Journal of John Wesley, Chapter 2, "I Felt My Heart Strangely Warmed," http://www.ccel.org/ccel/wesley/journal.vi.ii.xvi.html?highlight=strangely,warmed (accessed August 18, 2009).
3. H.B. London and Neil Wiseman, *Pastors at Greater Risk* (Ventura, Calif.: Regal, 2003), 58.
4. Ibid., 294.
5. Ibid., 282.

6. Jim Elliot, quoted by Trent Arwine in *Biography* 2009, http://amazingchrist.org/2009/06/the-seeking-life-jim-elliot/ (accessed August 18, 2009).
7. Gary McIntosh and Robert Edmondson, *It Only Hurts on Monday* (Carol Stream, Ill.: ChurchSmart Resources, 1998), 16.
8. Franklin Segler, *Christian Worship* (Nashville: Broadman & Holman Publishers, 1996), 240.
9. John Wesley, "Sermon XVI, The Means of Grace," in *The Works of John Wesley, Third Edition* (Kansas City, Mo.: Beacon Hill, 1979), 187–188.
10. John Mott, http://www.theoldtimegospel.org/dev/quote1.html (accessed August 23, 2009).
11. Philip Yancey, quoted in "Disappointment with God" at http://www.bgst.edu.sg/mmm/2003/2003issue5.htm (accessed August 18, 2009).
12. Oswald Chambers, quoted in "God's Greatest Desire" at www.intimacywithgod.com (accessed August 16, 2009).
13. E. M. Bounds, quoted at http://christianquotes.org/author/quotes/54 (accessed August 16, 2009).

Chapter 12

1. Elmer Towns, *An Inside Look at Ten of Today's Most Innovative Churches* (Ventura, Calif.: Regal Books, 1990), 28.
2. C. Kirk Hadaway and David A. Roozen, "Spiritual Revival on the Mainline," *The Christian Ministry*, Jan–Feb 1995, 27.
3. Elton D. Trueblood, *The Incendiary Fellowship* (New York: Harper & Row, 1967), 100.
4. Leonard Ravenhill, "Weeping Between the Porch and the Altar," http://www.ravenhill.org/weeping1.htm (accessed November 17, 2009).
5. Samuel Chadwick, *The Way to Pentecost* (Berne, Ind.: Light and Hope, 1937), 21.
6. Dwight L. Moody, http://www.brainyquote.com/quotes/quotes/d/dwightlmo165996.html (accessed November 17, 2009).

Chapter 13

1. Lynn Deshazo and Gary Sadler, "Let Your Fire Fall." © 1997 Integrity's Hosanna! Music.
2. William P. Mackay, "Revive Us Again." 1893 Public Domain. http://library.timelesstruths.org/music/Revive_Us_Again (accessed October 22, 2009).

Bibliography

Gangel, Kenneth & James Wilhoit. *Handbook on Spiritual Formation*. Grand Rapids, Mich.: Baker Book House, 1994.

Johnson, Todd E., ed. *The Conviction of Things Not Seen*. Grand Rapids, Mich.: Brazos Press, 2002.

Klein, Patricia S. *Worship Without Words*. Brewster, Mass.: Paraclete Press, 2007.

London, H.B., Jr. & Neil Wiseman. *Pastors at Greater Risk*. Ventura, Calif.: Regal Books, 2003.

McIntosh, Gary & Robert Edmondson. *It Only Hurts on Monday*. Carol Stream, Ill.: ChurchSmart Resources, 1998.

Morgenthaler, Sally. *Worship Evangelism*. Grand Rapids, Mich.: Zondervan, 1995.

Staples, Rob L. *Outward Sign and Inward Grace*. Kansas City, Mo.: Beacon Hill Press, 1991.

Tolson, Jay. "A Return to Tradition." *US News & World Report* (December 24, 2007).

Trueblood, Elton. *The Incendiary Fellowship*. New York: Harper & Row, 1967.

Walters, Michael. *Can't Wait for Sunday*. Indianapolis, Ind.: Wesleyan Publishing House, 2007.

Warren, Timothy. "The Purpose of Baptism," in *Leadership Handbooks of Practical Theology, Vol. 1*. Grand Rapids, Mich.: Baker Book House, 1992.

Webber, Robert. *Ancient-Future Time*. Grand Rapids, Mich.: Baker Books, 2004.

———. *Planning Blended Worship*. Nashville: Abingdon Press, 1998.

———. *Worship is a Verb*. Waco, Tex.: Word Books, 1985.

———. *Worship Old and New*. Grand Rapids, Mich.: Zondervan, 1982.